Date Due

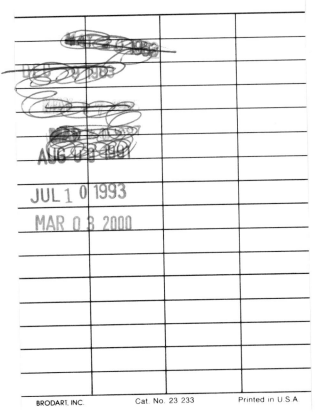

BRODART, INC.   Cat. No. 23 233   Printed in U.S.A.

YOUR GUIDE TO
A FINANCIALLY SECURE
RETIREMENT

Also by the Author

Dun & Bradstreet's Guide to Your Investments

Your Guide to
a Financially Secure
Retirement

C. COLBURN HARDY

HARPER & ROW, PUBLISHERS, New York
Cambridge, Philadelphia, San Francisco,
London, Mexico City, São Paulo, Sydney

1817

FIRST EDITION

Designer: Sidney Feinberg

Library of Congress Cataloging in Publication Data

Hardy, C. Colburn.
  Your guide to a financially secure retirement.
  Includes index.
  1. Finance, Personal.   2. Retirement income.
I. Title.
HG179.H283 1983   332.024′01   82–47525
ISBN 0–06–015034–3   AACR2

---

83 84 85 86 87 10 9 8 7 6 5 4 3 2 1

Contents

V. WHERE TO LIVE

Introduction

We spend so much time concentrating on the 10 to 20 percent of the elderly who have problems that we ignore the 80 to 90 percent who are independent, healthy and self-sufficient.

This statement is from remarks made before the White House Conference on Aging, in November 1981, by U.S. Senator Lawton Chiles, ranking minority member of the Special Committee on Aging. It is the theme of this book: *the majority of future retirees will (or can) look forward to comfortable, financially secure after-work years if* they plan wisely, save consistently, invest profitably, take advantage of opportunities and use common sense.

Right now, a retired couple, both aged 65, can count on assured annual income of close to $20,000, largely tax free *if* they make use of all of their assets. The real problem will be to keep ahead of inflation. But, again, this can be done when they set their minds, and resources, to it.

Better yet, prospects for a happy retirement are improving all the time. Those who quit work five or ten years from now can be even more optimistic if they set up their own Individual Retirement Accounts (IRAs).

From research, talks with knowledgeable authorities and personal observation, I am persuaded that at least 80 percent of all Americans now working can build financial security for their retirement years. The opportunities are there. In most cases, failure will be their own fault.

This optimism is in contrast to the dirges of many professional organizations and spokespersons for the elderly who harp and carp on the frail, impoverished minority of the already retired. These groups have been wailing so long that they have neglected the facts and have failed to realize the significant changes which have been, are now, and will be taking place in America's concern for senior citizens: Social Security indexed to inflation; growth of employer pension plans and the recent expansion of IRAs.

This guide to a financially secure retirement is written for that majority: the 80 percent to 90 percent of future retirees—the men and women now aged 45 to 60 who have the resources, will and discipline to effectively utilize all of their assets while working and after retirement and to recognize that what they do, or do not do, today will determine what they can, or cannot, do tomorrow.

There are, of course, people who cannot look forward to an enjoyable retirement. Some have not been able to earn enough money; others are not enrolled in pension plans; and most have not saved adequately or invested wisely. Fortunately, their numbers are dwindling as wages and salaries rise and benefits expand.

Consistent Progress

In this nation, we are often slow to develop solutions to major problems, but once the concepts have proven effective, we expand their scope and availability so that nearly everyone can benefit. It's easy to forget that the first step toward retirement security took place nearly fifty years ago: in 1937 with the start of Social Security. During World War II, private pensions became available to many more people, and since then, Congress has encouraged pensions through Keogh Plans, professional corporations plans and IRAs.

In 1974 Employee Retirement Income Security Act (ERISA) set standards, and in 1981 IRAs were expanded so that every wage earner can set up his/her own personal retirement program. The opportunities for a financially secure retirement are there for those who want to use them. Money alone won't assure successful after-work years, but it sure helps.

About This Book

Many of the examples in this book are presumed to be "typical" in that they predicate that both husband and wife are aged 65 and live their actuarially calculated life span. Such data should be considered only as a frame of reference.

Realistically, there are wide variations in retirees: wives three to five years younger than their husbands; an increasing number of singles due to divorce, death, or choice; double or triple pensions; more rewarding types of annuities; and, possibly soon, the elimination of penalties against Social Security for income earned after retirement.

There is also a growing number of people who do not fit established patterns: the 64-year-old retired New York City policeman who, for the past decade, has been working as a Florida tour guide; the retired harbor pilot who captains an Alaskan sightseeing motor vessel from mid-May to mid-September, then carves scrimshaw for the rest of the year; and the civil servant who moonlights as a newscaster at a local radio station and uses this income to set up his own pension plan.

In this book, I assume that the reader will:

1. Make necessary adjustments with his plans and calculations: saving more if he is older, less if he can hope for a substantial inheritance; projecting higher income if his spouse works and can count on a pension; lower income if she is fifteen years younger and not working

2. Take advantage of opportunities to build his/her own retirement assets through a pension plan at work and an IRA

3. Invest wisely for the most rewarding returns: switching to certificates of deposit (CDs) and money market funds when yields are high; back to discount bonds and common stocks when interest rates decline

4. Find out about legal and financial matters and make use of ideas and suggestions from knowledgeable experts

The Impact of Inflation

Since retirement deals with the future, inflation must be considered. As you'll learn, it is not as fearful as some doomsayers would have you believe and, usually, can work to your advantage. We've always had inflation in this country. The rate soared in recent years, primarily because of the oil crisis, but it is declining and, most experts predict, will soon settle to around 5 percent annually. That's a rate that can be handled with intelligent planning and investing . . . as will be explained.

Still, too many Americans assume that retirement is something for old folks, not for the young and middle-aged who are striving to get ahead. They fail to realize that it's later than they think.

If you are 45 years of age, you are already halfway through your working life. You still have time to build the assets you need.

If you're 55, you will be eligible for retirement in ten years. Adequate after-work income will require strict budgeting, substantial contributions to pension plans, profitable investments, and a bit of luck.

If you delay serious financial planning until age 60, you're in trouble. You will either have to inherit a bundle, win a lottery, keep working after 65, or, if you do retire, settle for a lower-than-welcome standard of living.

Background for This Book

This book stems from personal experience: my own early retirement; modest success in writing about investments and personal money management; lectures to working executives and professionals; and volunteer counseling to neighbors and friends.

With preretirees, I found that, while many had adequate resources, few had developed an organized approach to the management of their assets and even fewer realized the devastating impact of inflation. Only a handful had really projected their retirement income and after-work needs. *With retirees,* primarily Yale classmates and Florida neighbors, I found that there was greater understanding of inflation but, too often, a similar lack of financial planning. Some were worried; others were not sure of what to do; and still others were optimistic but wary of the future. They felt that they were no longer in control of their lives. As a consequence, they were slow or unwilling to adapt to changing conditions.

This became clear in the retirement community where we lived when we first moved to Florida. It was a self-contained unit: small houses, pool, clubhouse, recreation area and an active, well-managed homeowners' association. The residents could be divided into *old-timers* who had bought their homes when the project was opened ten years before and *newcomers* who had moved in more recently, primarily from the North. Some of the veterans were feeling a financial pinch; but, as they grew older, their expenses, especially for travel and recreation, were less because of physical limitations. Most of the "immigrants" were in good financial shape with ample nest eggs from the proceeds of the sale of their unmortgaged homes and the whopping yields of investments. There were, of course, some folks with problems.

I was asked to talk on investments and, soon, became a member of a team of lawyers and bankers who tried to help neighbors. This was an eye-opening experience. We found two types of situations: (1) failure to take advantage of investment opportunities—keeping what seems to me huge sums (often over $10,000) in low-yielding savings accounts rather than investing some of the funds in high-return CDs and money market funds; (2) insistence on retaining and even increasing assets for the benefit of heirs—a widow, living largely on Social Security, kept reinvesting some $4,000 interest income from a mutual fund scheduled to be left to her affluent son; a raggedly dressed widower who refused to borrow against or cash in a $100,000 life insurance policy with the named beneficiary a cousin whom he had not seen for twenty years.

Such experiences led me to research books on retirement. I found they could be divided into these categories:

- How to live after retirement: to keep busy, to become involved in community affairs, politics, etc. Some of these were interesting but not financially informative.
- Scholarly works on specific aspects of adult life: health, faith, family relations, and social attitudes.
- Personal commentaries on after-work living. These were occasionally entertaining, usually boring, and seldom of lasting value.
- How-to-get-ready-for books with charts, questionnaires, checklists, and so forth. Some were valuable, but, in most cases, the information was limited, general, and outdated.

This research convinced me that there was a need—and a market —for a fact-packed, tell-it-as-it-is guide to financing retirement. The original outline has been substantially revised, partly because of the extraordinary benefits to future retirees of the 1981 Economic Recovery Tax Act and partly because of new data developed after my appointment as a delegate to the White House Conference on Aging. The more I learned, the more convinced I became that the majority of people who retire from now on can count on a financially secure retirement. Lest this sounds too bullish, remember that most fears are never realized and, even then, seldom are as terrible as anticipated. Look back twenty years and see how often despair turned to joy. Look forward with enthusiasm and confidence.

There is, however, one caveat that will apply to a few: there can be problems when one or both partners live far beyond the actuarial life span. With inflation, fixed incomes buy less and less and there could come a time when capital will have to be invaded. *Do not panic.* All that this means is that you are making use of your savings rather than passing them on to your children.

Steps to Success

There is no one path to successfully financing retirement but, with few exceptions, everyone has to make choices between:

Spending for Needs Rather Than for Wants

Unless you are wealthy, spending must be keyed to needs rather than to wants. Only by having excess funds for investments, directly or indirectly in a pension/profit-sharing plan, will you be able to build the substantial assets needed for a financially secure retirement.

It sounds corny but there is still truth in the old fable of the gay, live-it-up-today grasshopper and the prudent, save-for-the-winter ant.

Investing for Growth or Income

If you invest solely for income you must pay substantial taxes and be willing to accept limited net returns, seldom sufficient to keep pace with inflation.

If you look for total returns—income plus appreciation—you will pay lower taxes, have more money to invest and can outpace inflation.

Investing or Speculating

If you invest on the basis of facts and proven corporate performance and keep reinvesting income, your savings will grow through the magic of compounding. If you risk your savings on hopes, tips or hunches, you are not likely to retain the assets needed for retirement.

Saving or Hoarding

Important as it is to save for retirement, it's foolish to stint yourself and your family in order to hoard more money than you will need to live comfortably after work. Even with inflation, it is difficult to spend much more than $25,000 (in today's dollars) a year in retirement, and you can't take it with you.

One final comment: *be realistic.* Your pension may seem secure; your anticipated Social Security payments attractive; but the best financial security is what you build for yourself through savings while you work and rewarding investments after you retire. Inflation is here to stay but it can work two ways. To a certain degree, it will always be destructive but, as you will learn in the pages ahead, there are ways it can be used constructively to enhance the value of your assets and help you to enjoy life after work.

I.
—

RETIREES
AND RETIREMENT

Because people are living longer senior citizens represent an increasing percentage of Americans. This creates problems but also opportunities. Retirement can be a welcome event for those who have the foresight to learn how to plan ahead: to develop personal interests, to review options on where to live and what to do, and to build financial assets.

Most future retirees can start with financial security if they make use of all of their assets and take advantage of pension plans. Inflation has been, and even at a lower rate, will continue to be annoying, but it also enhances values of property and returns on investments.

1. Retirees: America's Fastest-Growing Group

As a retiree, you will be part of the fastest-growing group in America. Senior citizens, defined as those over 65 years of age, now total over 24 million of the 220 million Americans. Their ranks are increasing by some 500,000 a year. By 1985, there will be 26.6 million; by the year 2000, 30.6 million. Roughly, 40 percent are and will be male, and 60 percent female.

Actually, the number of retirees is greater than that of senior citizens because, despite legislation that raised the mandatory quit-work age to 70, almost 70 percent of those drawing pensions and/or Social Security are under age 65. At major corporations that have excellent pension plans—Exxon and A.T.& T., for example—the average retirement age is under 60. But with inflation this trend is beginning to change, and more people are working longer.

Life span is increasing slowly so that the current actuarial table should be considered a minimum. At age 65, the life expectancy of a male is 14 years, to 79; that of a female is 18.4 years, to over 83. If your female ancestors were long-lived, chances are that you will beat those averages (table 1–1).

Relative Affluence

As will be repeated throughout this book, the majority of people who retire in and after 1982, will be financially secure. They can count on income from Social Security, savings and pensions, equal to 60 percent (or more) of their last working year's salary/wages.

Furthermore, nearly 80 percent of about-to-retire folks own their home, and an estimated 84 percent of these have paid off their mortgage; and 65 percent of families have savings/investments of over $20,000. To summarize a survey reported in *The New York Times* (9/10/80): "The negative image of the misfortunes of the elderly is

Table 1–1.   Life Expectancy

Age	Male	Female	Age	Male	Female	Age	Male	Female
55	20.8	26.4	65	14.0	18.4	75	8.6	11.5
56	20.1	25.6	66	13.4	17.7	76	8.2	10.9
57	19.3	24.7	67	12.8	16.9	77	7.8	10.3
58	18.6	23.9	68	12.2	16.2	78	7.4	9.8
59	17.9	23.1	69	11.6	15.5	79	7.1	9.3
60	17.2	22.3	70	11.1	14.8	80	6.7	8.8
61	16.5	21.5	71	10.6	14.1	81	6.4	8.3
62	15.8	20.7	72	10.1	13.4	82	6.1	7.9
63	15.2	19.9	73	9.6	12.7	83	5.8	7.5
64	14.6	19.2	74	9.1	12.1	84	5.5	7.1

SOURCE: Metropolitan Life Insurance Company; National Center for Health Statistics, Washington, D.C.

largely inaccurate. It has been reinforced by widespread news media coverage of a select few who may suffer from poverty, malnutrition, poor housing and serious health impairments. . . . When the non-cash benefits of Medicare, Medicaid, subsidized housing, Supplementary Security income (that guarantees a minimum income) and tax breaks are added to the higher retirement checks, only 6 percent of those over 65 can be considered poor."

And, let me add, the politically popular assertion that old folks are forced to eat pet food is false and absurd. Chicken is cheaper.

The Problem Is the Future

The real problem, and the one that should concern readers, is what's going to happen in the next twenty to thirty years of your lifetime. It's a mixed, somewhat scary, but generally bright picture.

On the one hand, pension benefits are rising because:

1. Social Security payments are indexed to the cost of living. In 1981, they went up 14 percent. The increases may be smaller in the future but, so far, Congress has clearly indicated they will not be eliminated.

2. Pensions are becoming better and more widely available. According to the President's Commission on Pension Policy, 48.1 percent of all active workers are covered by some sort of employment-based pension, profit-sharing or other type of retirement plan. But other surveys indicate that up to 70 percent of full-time workers are protected. And these reports were issued before the legislation was enacted permitting every wage earner to set up an Independent Retirement Account (IRA).

3. Under the provisions of the Employee Retirement Income Security Act (ERISA), full vesting (ownership)—where the employee has the right to receive all accumulated benefits at age 65—is becoming more

widely available. The act was passed in 1974 and, in many cases, mandates full vesting at the end of ten years. And there are strong pressures to improve these conditions.

On the other hand, there are problems that can limit, and possibly, eliminate some benefits: future Social Security payments may be taxed when total income is above certain levels (this will affect only the more affluent); some private pensions may be reduced, frozen, or, once in a while, never paid in full.

Increasingly, corporations are integrating Social Security with private pension plans. Since Social Security benefits are weighted in favor of low salary workers, private plans can, and usually do, allocate contributions and slant benefits to aid those who are paid more. The practical effect, says the American Association of Retired Persons, is to lessen the private pension benefits of low salary workers relative to the better paid. This is especially detrimental to women since their salaries average only 60 percent of men's compensation.

Today, the annual contributions for corporate pensions are approaching the after-tax profits of many companies. The time may come when, in order to compete and to maintain adequate profits, business may freeze or lower such allocations and thus limit corporate pension payments.

Already, many corporate pension plans have massive unfunded liabilities: i.e., they do not have the reserves needed to meet all future obligations and must rely on current contributions. In 1979, General Motors reported a short-fall of $3.9 billion in after-work commitments for its employees. Granted that this is somewhat of an accounting calculation and there is no indication that GM will cut or stop pension payments, but if one of the world's largest corporations has trouble, what about the thousands of smaller firms with limited resources?

There will be some protection through the Pension Benefit Guarantee Corporation. This federal agency can pay up to $750 per month to qualified employees of companies that go broke, move, or are merged. But the rate of funding, recently raised to $2.60 per corporate pension plan participant, is totally inadequate. If one major corporation, such as Chrysler Corporation, should fail, the benefits would require industry to pay at least $7 for each covered employee. By the time the money is collected and distributed, most of these retirees will be dead.

Social Security

Despite dire predictions, Social Security is not going to go broke. It involves too many people, is an integral part of our economic life, and has been one of the most successful government programs.

There will continue to be changes in the terms of qualification and benefits, but there is no reason for any retiree to expect to receive Social Security payments that are smaller than in the past or than officially projected for the future.

Social Security is a national commitment and will not only be preserved but, in some ways, enhanced. The financial troubles will be eased and, eventually, eliminated by congressional action.

Social Security's old age fund is a pay-as-you-go plan. The tax deductions from people at work provide the funds needed to pay those who are retired. The bite is getting bigger and before long, young people will be paying two or three times today's taxes for the same benefits their parents get now. In 1980, three workers supported one retiree. In thirty years, that ratio is expected to be two to one and, in fifty years, in theory anyway, there will be one worker for every retiree. Obviously, such a situation will not be popular and, probably, will be changed.

Other Data on Retirees

In after-work life there are important factors other than money. Some of their statistics relate to financial planning.

Age brings health problems. Retirees see their physician 50 percent more often and have twice as many hospital stays as younger people. One of every five senior citizens can expect to live in a nursing home for some period; four out of five have a chronic disease; 46 percent experience activity limitations because of physical ailments; and the suicide rate is the highest for any age group.

Still, with advances in medicine and treatments, most retirees will be able to avoid or, at least, lessen ill health. Even today, the situation is not as bad as some people fear: only 9 percent of all those over age 65 ever encounter medical situations and that 9 percent includes those who are in hospitals or institutions when they officially start retirement!

One factor can offset most of these dire forecasts: proper financial planning. According to a study by the College of Business Administration at the University of Oregon, there is a clear and favorable relationship between financial security and good health. Of those who planned for retirement:

• Over 50 percent reported generally good health in after-work years

- 75 percent do not worry about money (including those whose resources were limited)
- 85 percent are able to maintain their working lifestyle

And even more significant were the conditions/attitudes of those who either failed to plan for, or resisted, retirement:

- The majority were in poor health
- 26 percent were unable to adjust to retirement

Now do you see why financial planning for retirement is a total concept that involves money, health and lifestyle?

2. The Two Faces of Inflation

Whether you're a pessimist or optimist, you must consider inflation in your financial planning. The pessimists insist that continued inflation destroys individual savings, limits industrial expansion, bankrupts governments and will force an end of the free enterprise system as we know it.

The optimists point to the fact that most people have learned to adapt to inflation, that the worst is past and that once the official rate drops below 6 percent and the tax cuts take effect, there will be greater spendable income so that consumption will rise, more people will be working, productivity will improve and price increases will be minimal. And, they emphasize, "There must be something good about inflation because so many people seem to enjoy it."

The one sure point: inflation is here to stay and must be taken into account in all pre- and post-retirement planning.

Realistically, it seems to me, inflation has two faces: it does push up costs and lower purchasing power; but it also boosts returns on investments.

There's no question that the ever-rising costs of living have hurt and will continue to hurt those with fixed incomes and those with marginal earnings. The problems of both groups are more social than financial; the solutions involve government more than private or individual action: for the elderly, minimum Social Security, Medicaid, low cost meals, and special services; for younger people, food stamps, welfare, Aid to Dependent Children, etc.; and, for both, subsidized housing and transportation and tax breaks. There's room for improvement in many programs but, overall, both of these groups fare better now than they have in the past.

Since this book is about financing retirement and is keyed to a relatively affluent audience, the emphasis is on how to provide for comfortable, financially secure after-work years. For this group inflation is not now, nor will be, overly onerous.

In a survey of living costs from 1971 to 1978, the University of Michigan's Survey Research Center found that 54 percent of all families managed to stay ahead of inflation and that the per capita family income posted a 69 percent *real* income gain.

How Pessimists View Inflation

To show why you must consider inflation, let's start with the bad news: how costs of typical items have risen and may continue to rise—over a span of forty years, from 1962 to 2002 (table 2–1).

Table 2–1. How Costs Have Risen and May Continue to Rise

Item	1962	1982	1992	2002
One-family house	$19,200	$68,300	$158,748	$368,975
Standard four-door car	2,529	5,828	9,861	16,585
Refrigerator	470	530	575	650
Man's suit	130	238	349	512
Auto insurance premium	87	250	483	932
Electric bill (month)	8	40	75	150
Dinner out (for one)	4.65	10.95	18.70	31.94
Paperback book	.95	2.60	4.88	9.16
Movie ticket	.81	2.50	5.00	10.00
Hamburger	.28	.85	1.70	3.30
Candy bar	.05	.25	.68	1.88
First-class postage stamp	.04	.20	.35	.78

Source: Bureau of Census; Bureau of Labor Statistics; daily press.

The first twenty years are factual: from 1962 to 1982, the value of a one-family house jumped from $19,200 to $68,300; the price of a hamburger soared from 28 cents to 85 cents, etc. These increases took place when inflation rose to a record double-digit figure.

Using the same rate of inflation, the projections forecast that the same house will be worth $158,748 in 1992 and $368,975 in 2002, and the hamburger will cost $1.70 and $3.30, respectively. Those are awesome data!

But also note that there have been, and will be, exceptions to such ballooning: the refrigerator which cost $470 twenty years ago now sells for $530—$60 more. And its projected prices are only modestly higher: to $575 in ten years and to $650 after the turn of the century. These are modest premiums to pay for better quality and greater efficiency.

And while the table shows that automobiles could cost vastly more, this projection does not take into account the lower prices probable as the result of the wage/benefits concessions of the automobile industry. The point is that these are mechanical calculations which may be theoretically accurate but are impractical. They do not take into account man's remarkable ability to adapt, to improvise, to improve, and to economize.

Now let's do our own projections by using table 2–2 that shows the factor to use at various rates of inflation. To make these estimates, multiply the current cost/price/value by the appropriate figure under the selected rate of inflation for the number of years ahead: i.e., for 5 percent inflation, in ten years, 1.63; in twenty years, 2.65.

Table 2–2.   Inflation Factor at Annual Percentage Rate

Years	5%	6%	7%	8%	10%	12%
5	1.28	1.34	1.40	1.47	1.61	1.76
10	1.63	1.79	1.97	2.16	2.59	3.10
15	2.08	2.40	2.76	3.17	4.18	5.47
20	2.65	3.21	3.87	4.66	6.73	9.65

SOURCE: C. Colburn Hardy, *Your Money & Your Life,* American Management Association, New York, N.Y., 1982.

For a first-class postage stamp: multiply 20 by 1.63 to get 32.6 cents; by 2.65 to get 53 cents by 2002.

It's clear that to improve, let alone maintain your standard of living in the years ahead, you must organize yourself and family for the accumulation, conservation and distribution of your assets.

Now let's have some fun (and prick slightly the validity of both projections) by applying the factors to investment returns. Multiply the current 12 percent yield by 1.63 to get 19.56 percent in 1992 and by 3.21 to get a theoretical annual rate of return of 38.5 percent in 2002!

This points up why projections on future costs must be viewed with skepticism. Still, in the 1960s, the prime rate was 4.5 percent; Treasury bills paid 3.2 percent; bond coupons were around 4 percent; the highest dividends, from utility and bank stocks, were about 5 percent; *and inflation averaged* 1.5 percent; *a year.*

In early 1982 the prime rate was 15.75 percent; Treasury bills yielded 14 percent; long-term bonds paid 15 percent (and tax-exempt bonds nearly as much); and inflation was below 10 percent and heading down. And, even more important for readers of this book, tax rates are decreasing and opportunities for savings increasing. Inflation has been, and will be, significant, but it is not as bad as many people think and proclaim.

The "True" Rate of Inflation

The official rate of inflation is determined by the Consumer Price Index (CPI), but this has not been an accurate measure of individual costs as is indicated by the fact that, in mid-1982, there will be substantial revisions, primarily in the weight given to housing and the criteria used for food costs. Under the old CPI:

• Housing costs, which accounted for about 10 percent of the index, were based on the assumption that every American bought a new house every month with a mortgage at the then current rate of interest.

• The food costs were based on 1972–73 prices when the price of beef was comparatively low and a major consumer purchase. But in a few years, the price of beef rose sharply and people turned to lower-cost chicken. This change in buying habits was not reflected in the CPI.

Most experts anticipate that, with the new CPI, the stated rate of inflation will be closer to 5 percent than to the recent 10 percent. From my research, I suspect that a 5 percent inflation rate is the maximum that should be used to project future costs. If you're a pessimist, use a higher figure, but do so only after analyzing your own budgets on a year-by-year, item-by-item basis.

At this rate, preretirees should be able to stay ahead of inflation and postretirees will do O.K. with proper planning and wise use of their assets. Here's why:

Most workers get raises more or less keyed to the cost of living, so their income will keep pace. With merit raises, they will stay ahead. Since federal income taxes will be lower and, by 1985, will probably be relatively stable because of the higher personal exemptions, the majority of working Americans will beat inflation.

For older, getting-ready-to-retire people, some major outlays remain static or can be reduced: mortgage payments, premiums on life insurance and interest on installment loans.

When a family budgets and watches its expenses, it can maintain for a surprisingly long time about the same dollar expenditures: by buying hamburger instead of steak; by driving cars less and longer; by shopping for bargains; and by doing it yourself. This is easier when there are no longer children at home and, in retirement, can be part of the challenge of everyday living.

And the costs of many widely used items are declining: air fares, electronic products, banking services, and so on.

For retirees who plan ahead, inflation should be even less damaging. If they bought major items while working, there will be no major expenditures for many years. When they do have to buy replacements, such outlays can be met by continuing a savings program.

Inflation Boosts Income

This is repeated because it is a factor that is often overlooked. Inflation almost always increases value and, often, income. Let's say you are making $20,000 a year and that your pay rises 6 percent annually (a combination of cost of living and merit). Using table 2–2, multiply the twenty-year factor to find your future salary twenty years hence, when you plan to retire: 3.21 × $20,000 = $64,200 future salary.

If you retire at that time, and both you and your spouse are 65, Social Security, based on projections from the table, will be $29,150 a year (again, using that 5 percent inflation factor). Now let's be conservative and set your corporate pension at 25 percent of your last year's income: $16,050. That means that, hopefully, you will quit work with assured lifetime income of $45,200. That's just about the $45,150 representing 75 percent of your last working year's salary.

It should be easy to bridge the most gaps and to build extra protection with personal savings, preferably an IRA. Now do you see why inflation is not as debilitating as it may seem?

Of course, there's no guarantee that such pay increases will take place or that your corporate pension will be as much, but these are *logical, fact-based projections.*

To make your own calculations on how to stay ahead of inflation with investments, use table 2–3.

Pensions

Pension plans can also benefit from inflation when their benefits are tied to inflation (they are covered in chapter 00). In some cases, retirees receive more money than they did while working, as do many government workers who benefit from "comparability." Initiated by the federal government in 1968, it involves a complex formula that relates

Table 2–3:   How to Figure After-Tax, After-Inflation Break-Even Point

What counts is what's left after deducting taxes and recognizing the erosion of purchasing power due to inflation. To find the break-even point for return on investments, use this formula:

$$\frac{IR}{INV\text{-}TR} = BE$$

IR = Inflation rate
INV = $ investment in units of 10
TR = Tax rate
BE = Break-even point

You anticipate that inflation will be 5 percent next year; you pay federal income taxes at a 37 percent tax rate; your investment base is $1,000. To *break-even,* your savings must earn 7.9 percent:

$$\frac{5}{100 - 37} = \frac{5}{63} = 7.9 \text{ percent}$$

With long-term capital gains, where only 40 percent of the profits are taxed, in that same 37 percent tax bracket, the tax rate would be 15 percent (rounded out). Thus, the *BE* for after-one-year profits would be 5.9 percent.

This formula applies to personal investments, not to those in tax-advantaged pension plans.

When inflation is higher, the necessary yields will have to be much greater—as has been the case in recent years.

retirement income to the salary paid for the position from which the individual retired and to inflation.

Example: In 1968 Phil V. started work as a middle management Civil Service employee at $22,000 a year. In the next 4½ years, the inflation factor would have raised his pay about 22 percent (to $26,840) but under the weighted formula, it spurted over 50 percent to $34,971, with no promotions. If Phil had continued to work until 1980, his salary, for the same job, would have been more than $50,000 annually.

Fortunately for Phil, he took early retirement in July 1975 with an annuity of $23,064 a year. But, based on the index, his benefits, by 1980, rose to $36,900 . . . and, with twice a year indexing, continued to increase.

What to Do

For most people, however, beating inflation is a personal challenge. It can be met, and usually overcome, by wise planning and by personal savings, preferably through an IRA. After ten years of such tax-deductible savings, every $100 contribution will provide lifetime income of

$235—when the average yield is 12 percent a year.

Another note of cheer: the value of your house, at retirement, will be at least double, and probably, triple, its cost. With the mortgage paid off, you'll have money enough to buy a smaller home and be able to invest a sizeable sum.

Housing prices may not rise as rapidly as they have in the past decade, but their values will increase (unless there's a severe depression). Housing prices reflect anticipation of higher prices in the future so that as long as there's hope, they should keep moving up and make retirement that more rewarding.

Warning: The one big problem with inflation, after retirement, is life span. With proper planning, most people can be sure of adequate income as long as they can be expected to live—actuarially. But if you, or your spouse, outlive the average, there could be trouble. At age 90 —eleven years longer than the expectancy for a male and six years longer than that for a female at age 65—the erosion of inflation could be harmful unless you are willing to invade capital.

With all calculations/projections, the assumption is that one or both partners will live average length lives. If, by heredity or personal confidence, you believe you will be an exception, add to your savings while you are still working!

II.

——

FINANCIAL PLANNING
BEFORE RETIREMENT

To achieve any goal, you must set a target. For retirement, that means financial security: enough assets to provide enough income to meet the lifelong needs of you and your spouse and, ultimately, one individual. Success requires consistent savings, rewarding investments and utilization of all of your resources.

If you play while you work and fail to set aside reserves for the future, you will have trouble. But if you set up, and adhere to, a plan, your future will be safe and sure. *What you do or do not do while working will determine what you can or cannot do after you retire.*

3. How Much Money You Will Need

Financial planning for retirement should start early, ideally a few years after you start your first job, have your debts under control and are able to save a few dollars regularly. The best rule is to save as much as you can, to take advantage of tax-favored pension or profit-sharing plans and to invest for maximum, safe total returns.

Specific planning for the kind of retirement life you want to live should be delayed until you begin to think seriously about quitting work, occasionally in your mid-50s but, usually, after your sixtieth birthday.

As a first step, pencil in answers on the activity chart (see table 3–1). Do this separately, without consultation with your spouse. Review these, again alone, a month later and make revisions. Finally, compare your projections and, together, prepare a larger, more detailed checklist. The husband might leave the first two spaces blank while the wife might write down, under Hobby, wood-carving and, under Craft, flower arranging. These reflect serious thought because the first will be best for winter and the second for summer. Be imaginative. Hope and dream a little, even if some of the ideas seem unusual. Retirement should be a time when you can do what you want to do when and how you want to do it!

Once you have developed a broad framework, set aside a Sunday afternoon to discuss each item with emphasis on physical limitations and probable costs. Your choices will depend a good deal on whether you plan to stay in your hometown or move away. If you have been active in your place of worship, the chances are that you will have to give this a high priority as an alert minister/priest/rabbi will target you or your spouse for an important committee. If you move, there will be no such responsibilities and volunteer work can be on your own terms.

Limit your list to activities you plan for the first five years of retirement. By age 70, most people slow down. This caveat applies especially

Table 3–1.　How Will You Spend Your Time in Retirement?

What I Want to Do	What I'll Need	Estimated Cost	Rewards/Satisfactions
Hobby			
Craft			
Sports			
Community service			
Club/Church or synagogue			
Education			
Travel			
Job: full-time			
Job: part-time			
Professional activities			
Other			

to travel, so mark trips according to your joint priorities with the most wearing and expensive checked no. 1 and no. 2.

If you enjoy a close relationship with your children or other members of your family, ask their help and heed their counsel. They should know you both well and be able to make candid and meaningful comments.

Once you have a fairly set list, start implementation. With hobbies and crafts, go to night school to learn to paint or build furniture and buy the tools and equipment you will need. Go slowly when these items are expensive, your health is such that you may not be physically able to pursue those dreams or you are already on a tight budget.

Finally, review the list every year and add or delete in accordance with your changing interests and anticipated income.

If you have a hard time filling out this activity chart, work backward. List those projects that you do *not* like, in which you do *not* feel competent and those that you feel will be difficult to work out: i.e., becoming involved with real estate because of the requirements for substantial cash outlays and continuing responsibilities.

N.B. Unless you have specific prior experience, do not plan to become an after-work millionaire by buying property with nothing down, fixing it up and selling out for a handsome gain. Despite the numerous books on the subject, such real estate successes are rare. In most cases, it's more rewarding, and fun, to enjoy retirement.

Getting Help

Until a few years ago, retirement was a simple process. Each corporate/government retiree was called into the personnel office, given a few basic facts about Social Security and pension and, a couple of months later, sent out into the world with a "Good luck" handshake and, now and then, a testimonial luncheon.

Today, retirement, especially from major corporations, is a full-fledged program. Many companies provide preretirement counseling through seminars that involve employees and their spouses. These organized sessions feature experts on financial planning, estate planning, health maintenance and on outlining ways to increase leisure time happily and productively. Make sure you attend them, take notes and reread the literature.

At every step of your planning, be sure that one of you keeps a clear head and recognizes that, in most cases, after-work lifestyle will be similar to that to which you are accustomed. Only rarely do people change significantly after they stop work. The *doers* keep on doing and the *don'ters* keep on minding their own business. The woman who has devoted her life to caring for her family and has limited her outside interests to her luncheon and bridge clubs seldom takes up painting or golf or attends college.

And the man who, for thirty-nine years, left home at 7:50 A.M. and returned at 5:50 P.M. to eat, listen to the radio or watch TV and join a once-a-week poker party is not about to run for city council or become an ardent bicyclist. That's O.K. Everyone is an individual and should have the opportunity to live in the style that he/she enjoys or, at least, is comfortable with.

Yet, regardless of your working life background, do try to retire *into* something, not *out* of a job. Be willing to unfreeze established behavior patterns if only a trifle. You may be surprised at how exciting it can be to carve a toy, polish a stone and set it in a bracelet or attend courses on American history.

One suggestion: try to set up activities that will maintain or attract friendships. Half the fun of gardening is exhibiting your flowers at the local shows or bringing bouquets and plants to patients in the hospital.

Schedule your trips to include visits to old friends. If you plan to rent a camper to see America, get the addresses of college classmates and fellow employees who have moved away, drop them a note or Christmas card and, when retirement comes, route your trips so you can see them. There will be some no-replies and a few rebuffs, but most of the folks will be glad to see you, especially when you assure them that you have your own sleeping quarters or plan to stay in a motel.

Now that you have some idea of life after work, let's see how much money you will need to enjoy these retirement years.

Gauging Your Financial Needs

As a rule of thumb, you will need 75 percent to 60 percent of your last working year's income for a reasonably comfortable retirement. The exact amount will depend on:

Your anticipated lifestyle. If you are one of those rare individuals who wants to get away from it all and heads for the South Seas or the Maine woods, your expenses will be far lower than if you chose a populated area. If you splurge on travel, you'll need more money, especially if your spouse insists on staying at a first-class hotel in London where $100 a day is a minimum charge.

Your responsibilities (financial aid to your children or relatives, health care costs, etc.). If you remarry at age 50 and have children, you probably will not be able to stop work at 65, so you will be retired for a shorter time.

The age at which you retire. If you have fifteen years to go, you can assume that you will be earning more by age 65 and, hopefully, your income will go up faster than inflation. And your pensions can be greater.

Your assured income. Not only the dollars you receive every month but also those which can be drawn from capital.

From scores of surveys, personal observation and comments by professional counselors, I believe that most people who will retire in the future can get along comfortably on that 75 percent and, with determination, discipline and smart money management can make out at that 60 percent level. Most people can also supplement their fixed income by part-time work or self-employment.

Not everyone will adjust quickly but in two or three years, normal outlays can be cut substantially. Do not expect miracles. A few of these economies will come easily; some will take time; and others will be forced by limited funds or physical handicaps.

Once you know your assured income, you can build an after-work budget. In most cases, this will be easier than you anticipate if only because, in retirement, you have time to learn how to cut expenses: do-it-yourself projects at home; planning meals and trips to get more for your dollar; riding a bicycle or car pooling with neighbors; and taking advantage of the many money-saving opportunities available to those over 65. When there's a will, there's usually a way.

There are still two financial perils:

1. *The death of the primary breadwinner.* This can decrease income

sharply: about one-third for Social Security and partially or completely with employer pensions. The survivor can live on less but in all retirement planning, it is essential to think of long-term needs after the death of one partner, usually the husband.

2. *That persistent bugaboo—inflation.* While you are working, there can be some protection through salary increases, but, with the fixed incomes of most retirees, there is little chance to escape. For a while it is possible to cut expenses—to buy cheaper cuts of meat, to patch or recut clothes, to cancel subscriptions to one newspaper and a few magazines in the same category and to limit restaurant meals to "early bird specials." But, eventually, there will be a point of resistance beyond which you will have to make major changes: get a part-time job, move to cheaper quarters, or take in boarders.

Still, to repeat: inflation is not as bad as some people project, especially when you plan ahead. Some costs will remain static; others will, or can be, decreased; and the values of some assets will rise and can be utilized more effectively.

One more important point: income taxes after work will be lower, often nil. All Social Security payments (which represent about half of after-work income for most people) are tax exempt (but may be partially taxed in the future); a portion of many private pensions is tax free as a return of capital; and tax benefits are available with Tax Savers Certificates and certain utility stocks and municipal bonds. As a rule of thumb, retired couples do not pay federal income taxes until their after-work income is about $20,000 a year.

Retirement Budgets

Using that 75 percent figure, the couple who has been spending $25,000 a year can live comfortably, after work, on $18,750 but, for easy figuring, let's set that budget at $20,000.

With 5 percent annual inflation, that $20,000 will rise to about $25,600 in five years; to $32,600 in ten years and to $41,600 in fifteen years. These are awesome projections but, practically, these are overly pessimistic. Still, it's a good idea to keep those figures in mind in your financial planning.

Budgets should be frames of references—no more. The actual expenditures will vary with personal priorities and methods of allocation: cleaning supplies may be included with Housing or listed under Furnishings. Some expenditures will depend on where and how you choose to live: transportation costs will be low if you live in a city or close to a shopping center. If you live in an apartment or condominium, you won't have to pay for garden supplies or maintenance.

Table 3–2 shows a budget for a couple who can count on $20,000 a year: Social Security of about $11,000; pensions of $5,000 and savings/investment income of $4,000. In five years, their income, with Social Security rising at a modest 5 percent a year (far less than it has been recently), will rise to $23,000. In ten years, even with a lower return on investments, the available funds will total $26,000.

Table 3–2.   Budget for Retired Couple: 5 Percent Annual Inflation

Item	Percent at Start	Year 1	Year 5	Year 10
Housing/utilities	30	$ 6,000	$ 7,200	$ 8,500
Food/liquor/meals out	20	4,000	5,200	6,200
Furnishings/garden	4	800	700	1,200
Clothes	5	1,000	1,000	800
Transportation	8	1,600	2,000	1,800
Medical/dental	8	1,600	2,000	2,500
Recreation/travel	11	2,200	2,100	2,000
Insurance	1	200	200	200
Gifts/contributions	3	600	600	700
Taxes (federal/state)	1.5	300	300	200
Personal	2.5	500	500	600
Miscellaneous	3.5	700	800	900
Savings*	2.5	500	400	400
Total	100%	$20,000	$23,000	$26,000

* Reserve fund to be used for emergencies and replacements

Source: Bureau of Labor Statistics and Florida Council on Aging and Adult Services (of which I am a member).

Before you scoff at these figures as unrealistic, let me quote from the data used by the U.S. Department of Labor as expenses of a typical retired couple. These figures were based on 1979 data so should be updated by multiplying by 1.2 to reflect the recent rates of inflation.

	1979	1982
Lower budget	$ 6,644	$ 8,637
Intermediate budget	9,434	12,264
Higher budget	13,923	18,099

The last figure comes close to that base $20,000 shown in the budget of table 3–2. It's a bit higher than the national average because the audience to which this book is addressed will, or can be somewhat more affluent than the average. If you project that your after-work income will be lower, adjust the figures by reducing the items for taxes, gifts, transportation and recreation/travel.

Most people dislike the shackles of a budget but some sort of financial control is essential in retirement because spending can easily get out of hand, and with limited opportunities to boost income, you will have to curtail some of the anticipated pleasures.

The base for a retirement budget should be started three years before you quit work by:

• Buying and paying for major items, such as appliances, furniture, automobiles, tools/hobby equipment.

• Repairing/remodeling your home if you plan to stay there.

• Repaying all debts unless they are on unusually favorable terms: a mortgage with a 10 percent rate of interest; a loan against a life insurance policy at 6 percent with the proceeds invested for a 12 percent yield.

• Completing or updating all legal documents: wills, trusts, etc.

Think of retirement as the start of a new business or, to some degree, the beginning of a new type of living.

These sample budgets are worked backward in that the expenditures are based on assured income. But the percentages for the categories are, relatively, accurate in that they represent a composite of data from governmental agencies, private, money-oriented organizations and personal experience: my own and that of neighbors and classmates. But there can be significant variations depending on location, personal preferences, lifestyle and resources.

In developing your own budget, start with your current annual expenditures, take out the capital items, eliminate the taxes (no more deductions for Social Security and withholding) and pension contributions; reduce the amounts for clothing, transportation and insurance; then calculate your percentages. The results should be close to those of table 3–2.

Once you have established that framework, try to keep fairly accurate records of expenditures. If you dislike detail, work against your cancelled checks and sales receipts and set up a special file for "Unknown." When this category becomes substantial, reallocate costs arbitrarily, and try to do better in the next quarter.

After retirement, review the budget every three months but do not make any major changes until the end of the first year. One big month's expenditures for car repairs may be followed by low costs for transportation for the rest of the year. This sounds elementary but, I found, often sparks unnecessary fears and arguments. Watch for trends of over- and underspending. These can develop slowly . . . but, sad to say, surely.

This proposed budget makes certain, well-founded assumptions that:

- The mortgage is, or soon will be, paid off.
- With age, many expenses will decline. You'll be driving less; your vacations will be shorter; and you'll be entertaining less frequently.
- You will make internal switches to accommodate special needs: more money for a European vacation one year and less when you stay home the next. (But in the future it will be more.)
- Medical expenses will be reduced by Medicare. On the average, Medicare picks up 40 percent of the tab so that total costs of $2,000 will end up as $1,200 on the budget.
- Insurance costs will remain at the same $200 even though, in most cases, the premiums will drop because policies will be paid up or reduced by dividends. This gives you extra leeway.

Professional Comments

To present a more or less impartial overview of these budgets, I checked with a professional consultant who made these comments:

Housing/utilities. This is the largest and most-difficult-to-handle item. For many people, ownership of a home is an emotional, not a financial, decision. Staying in the big old house provides a sense of security. This is fine as long as you can afford it. But if maintenance/comfort costs become too high, you will have to sacrifice/economize in other areas.

After work, total housing costs should not run more than 30 percent of your sure income. If your projections show a higher figure and this proves correct in the first year, there can be trouble.

Before you decide to move, make every effort to reduce costs, especially those of heating and/or air-conditioning. Ask your local utility company to make a survey and show you how to lower bills by adjusting your water heater, adding insulation or scheduling washing at off-peak hours—easily done now that you can be home all day.

If these savings are not enough (and, usually, they will be temporary alleviants), you will have to make that all-important choice: to rent rooms, bring in someone else to help defray expenses or sell. With rare exceptions, there will be a pleasant profit from the sale of the old homestead, and, in all cases, there will be no taxes on the first $125,000 of capital gain. And nearly 80 percent of all older couples own their home mortgage free.

It may be difficult to sell your home, psychologically, but, usually, it will be a wise decision financially. With the proceeds, you can buy, or rent, a new home and still have a substantial sum to invest for extra income. With housing costs, more than almost any other major expenditure, there are viable alternatives.

Food/liquor/meals out. This category is flexible and subject to greater economies than almost any other type of expenditure. That's why the projections, five and ten years hence, show small increases. When you have extra time—and are willing to make an extra effort—there are scores of ways to save money with food and related items:

• Buy fresh vegetables instead of convenience foods. They are cheaper and, usually, better tasting.

• Can fresh vegetables. It's fun and can save a bundle.

• Before you go to the supermarket, check the ads, save the coupons and watch for double coupon-value days, plan meals for a week and make a detailed shopping list.

• Shop alone as there's less chance for costly impulse buying.

• Do not shop when you are tired or hungry. Under such conditions, you'll buy too many of the wrong, and usually unnecessary, items.

• When you dine out, go early and take advantage of "early bird specials."

Finally, as you'll soon learn, the older you get, the less you eat . . . and drink.

Transportation. If you're like most people, your new freedom will boost these costs at the outset of retirement (unless you've been commuting quite a distance to work).

With few specific commitments, it's easy—and a welcome change of pace—to hop in the car when you need something or when you go out, to meander around, visit new shopping centers, drop by old neighborhoods, and, generally, waste gasoline. Driving the car becomes more of an enjoyable luxury than a necessity.

But you can save a mint when you set your mind to it: planning shopping trips; car pooling with neighbors; using public transportation (almost all trains and buses offer lower fares for senior citizens and many communities have special vans that go to medical centers and recreation areas).

If you're still adventuresome, buy a moped. If you're cautious, get a bicycle. And when there are few or small packages, walk. The exercise will do you good, and you can chat with old and new friends along the way.

There can also be big savings with your automobile(s). You have time to wash and polish, change the oil, and if you're mechanically inclined, keep the engine in top shape.

Here again, preplanning is important. If you plan to take long trips, buy a large car. The costs will be higher but you'll be more comfortable. By trade-in time—after you've passed age 70—you'll probably prefer to stay closer to home so a small car will be satisfactory . . . and less expensive. You can always rent a station wagon for special occasions. As one retired auto dealer told me, "Despite higher prices for fuel and repairs, my total transportation costs, including a trade-in for a new compact, are less today—eight years after retirement—than they were when I stopped work."

This is a rather verbose commentary but points out how and why inflation, in terms of dollars, need not be a major threat to most retirees.

Medical/dental. This is the most difficult-to-project cost of retirement. If you, or your spouse, become ill, these expenses can skyrocket. But the odds are at least eleven to one that such a dire situation will not occur!

Almost all older people do . . . or will . . . have physical ailments. In most cases, they will be more irritating than costly. Realistically, if there is a serious illness, there's not much you can do about it.

The payments you must make before Medicare takes over will continue to rise, but on the average, this health insurance can be expected to pay about 40 percent of your medical/hospital bills.

My mother, who lived to age 94, was in the hospital three times during her last five years. Yet her total out-of-pocket medical expenses were less than $3,000—well below this budget.

Unfortunately, there are two costly areas: dental care and nursing homes. Unless you are lucky enough to be able to carry over dental insurance into retirement, these expenses can be onerous.

With nursing homes, there can be some aid from insurance and Medicare, but the only favorable fact of such confinements is that other living expenses will be minimal.

Statistically, health-related costs become burdensome for retirees primarily when they live beyond their actuarial age and have a previous history of ill-health. These budget figures represent averages so if you and/or your spouse are fearful, increase this category and make reductions elsewhere.

Or, better yet, set aside, mentally or actually, a portion of your savings/investments for future medical needs. *But do not stint your lifestyle because of fears alone.* Enjoy retirement as long and as fully as you can. We are all familiar with sad tales of the ill elderly, but it is important to remember that they involve only a small percentage of retirees. Most senior citizens can count on a long, reasonably healthy, financially secure retirement.

Recreation/Travel. This is the most flexible item. How much you spend depends more on lifestyle and physical abilities than on available dollars. In the first years, you'll probably want to travel, but by the time you're in your 70s, the thrill will be gone either because of physical ailments or the desire of one partner to get home.

If you like to travel abroad, schedule your trips off-season to take advantage of the lower rates, and if you splurge one year, skip the next.

With recreation, it's important to plan ahead. If you enjoy golf, pick a community built around, or close to, a course. Here, too, time will take its toll. The retiree who, at age 66, walked a daily round will settle for playing twice a week, with a cart, at the age of 72.

Insurance. This is another item that, in most cases, can be eliminated. If you can afford to retire, you have assured income so there's no longer need to provide for replacement at your death. But if you anticipate that your spouse will lose your pension, keep enough life insurance to bridge this gap. Roughly, this means $10,000 protection for $1,500 annual payment.

If you own straight life, the premiums will be fully or largely paid for by the dividends. And don't forget that if you have borrowed against the cash value of a policy, the loan will be deducted from the death benefit.

This $200 a year is budgeted because, psychologically, many people, especially wives, want the security of the death benefit so that there will be ample cash to pay for the costs of final illness, burial, and settlement of the estate. After retirement, life insurance is a better security blanket than investment.

Gifts/contributions. This is another item that can be reduced or eliminated when there are financial pressures. It represents community/personal commitments: to your place of worship, United Way, hospital, college, etc.—not to your family. In most cases, contributions will be much lower than those made while you were working.

If you stay in the same community, such cuts will be difficult so set this part of your budget at the beginning of the year and make your choices carefully on the basis of genuine interest rather than social/political pressures. You've already paid your dues, and it's time that more of the burden of support is turned over to those better able to afford it.

Gifts to your family should be made only from excess assets, not as a regular commitment.

Taxes. This category is for income taxes and, in a few states, for the intangible tax on investments. In states, or cities where there are local levies, the total may be higher but, again, with proper planning, the federal tax bite should be small. With the $20,000 income, not more than $8,000 will be taxable. Since a couple, both over age 65, starts with a $7,400 deduction on their federal return, that leaves only $600 as a tax base. From this can be deducted interest, real estate taxes, sales taxes, dividend exemptions, etc. There may be some state or local levies, but for most retirees, direct taxes are not a significant cost of living.

Personal/Miscellaneous are catch-all categories. Use them for costs of beauty/hair care, cosmetics, newspapers and magazines and anything that cannot be easily allocated elsewhere. And if these expenditures mount beyond the budget, review the situation immediately. After work, dimes become as important as dollars were when you had a regular paycheck.

Savings. This should be listed as a reserve account. These savings are for near-future use: to pay for unexpected home and car repairs, to replace bedsheets and dishes, to join friends on a vacation weekend or to make a trip to visit your new grandchild. These monies should be invested for extra income: at best, in high-yielding money market funds; at worst, in a savings account. Be cautious about using these funds to buy stocks or bonds because their values may be down when you need the money.

Warning: Do not continue the same rate of savings as you did while working. Retirement is the time to spend those hard-earned assets. Too many people continue to set aside substantial sums from force of habit, or fear. In most cases, this is foolish. Some folks seem to believe that they will live forever but only half of us will beat the actuarial tables. Death can come suddenly and large savings will be wasted—at least as far as the deceased is concerned.

One of my friends who is an officer of a local thrift institution tells me that over half of elderly depositors continue to save as much in retirement as they did when they had regular incomes. Setting aside $100 a month may be comforting but cannot be justified when either you or your spouse needs a new set of dentures or you have to skip your college Class Day.

Survivor's Budget

Once you have established a fairly firm and viable budget for a couple, it's time to be a pessimist and assume that one of you will die soon. Actuarially, it will be the husband so table 3–3 outlines a budget for a widow. It assumes that: (1) death will not occur until after five years of retirement; (2) the income will be 75 percent of previous income; and (3) inflation will be 5 percent annually. Thus, the budget is $15,410 after five years of retirement; $17,420 after ten years.

Here again, this is worked backward from the base income: Social Security, cut by one-third; no more pension and slightly higher income from savings/investments due to the assets of the estate after payment of all bills: at the outset, plus $2,010 representing a 10 percent yield on $20,000; later, plus $2,420 due to a small invasion of capital.

Obviously, if the inheritance is less, there will have to be economies. But there is an extra reserve because the house could be sold and the widow (or widower) could rent or buy a smaller home and spend or invest the balance.

Table 3–3.   **Budget for Widow: 75 Percent of Previous Income; 5 Percent Inflation**

Item	After Retirement	
	5 Years	10 Years
Housing/utilities	$ 6,800	$ 7,200
Food/liquor/meals out	3,800	4,200
Furnishings/garden	400	600
Clothes	700	800
Transportation	900	900
Medical/dental	1,010	1,500
Recreation/travel	1,000	1,000
Gifts/contributions	200	200
Personal	400	500
Miscellaneous	400	520
Total	$15,410	$17,420

Based on these sources of income (rounded out): Social Security indexed at 5% annually.

Social Security	$9,400	$12,000
Savings/investments	6,010	5,420
Total	$15,410	$17,420

SOURCE: Social Security Administration; U.S. Department of Labor; White House Conference on Aging. (Composite)

If the couple planned well, there will be adequate assets to support the survivor past age 75. With an actuarial life span of eleven years, the widow can start drawing on capital. She should be cautious about taking out a large lump sum as this will leave less money to earn income. She can always boost the payout. In autumn years, an extra few hundred dollars can mean the difference between comfort and subsistence. And, she can't take it with her!

Yes, there is a minimum level of income needed for comfortable retirement, but with wise financial planning before and after work, this will be reached only if you or your spouse far outlive actuarial tables or start out with minimal income and assets (which, of course, means you fail to heed the advice in this book).

What to Do

When you find a wide gap between your current expenses and the budget projected for retirement, start making revisions.

In the futures budget, by setting fixed limits for expenses: i.e., a flat $3,000 a year for travel and entertainment and $2,000 for transportation. This will mean you will have to forego some dreams but you can always hope for a windfall: an inheritance or a big capital gain from the sale of company stock bought while you were working. Or you can assure lower transportation costs by buying your new home close to a shopping center.

In your current budget, by careful planning, either by setting fixed limits, implementing an across-the-board slash or increasing your savings.

If you are an optimist, make new calculations with inflation at a lower rate. As you remember from past experience—when the kids were in college or before your spouse went back to work—you can get along on less if you have to!

Warning: Do not set impossible limits on reduced budget items. If you cut down too far on food, there can be health problems. If, as head of the house, you mandate no more new clothes for six months, there's bound to be family controversy.

It's better to use ranges, stay flexible and space economies: steak every two weeks instead of every Sunday; spending one week of vacation at home; or slip-covering the couch instead of buying a new one. Money is not the only thing, and what you feel are logical economies can cause emotional strains for others.

Estimating Your Own Retirement Expenses

To provide a base for future planning, use table 3–4. This is valuable *only* for broad projections of total anticipated expenses when you start retirement. The actual allocations will shift after work to reflect changes in lifestyle: *up* for recreation/travel (at the outset); *down* for life insurance, income taxes and savings/investments.

This table is included at the suggestion of a professional counselor who says, "The idea that you can live for 25 percent less is intriguing to most people but they do not realize the impact of inflation or just how the reductions will be achieved. Too often, they guesstimate the savings will automatically permit them to boost expenses for travel and eating out. Unfortunately, it seldom works out that way. By keeping a table like this up to date, they won't be surprised when they retire. And if inflation is less than anticipated, things will be easier."

In column (1), write down your current expenditures. If you do this early in the year, work with the data collected for your income tax return. Don't worry about being accurate to the last dollar and add an asterisk when there were unusual outlays. Over the years, items tend to even out.

In column (2), put down 75 percent (or 60 percent) of the column (1) figure: i.e., if the shelter total is $8,000, pencil in $6,000 or $4,800.

Column (3) is the most important for planning because it projects

Table 3–4.   Estimating Retirement Expenses

Item	Current (1)	After Retirement Percentage of (1) (2)	After Inflation 5 Years	10 Years (3)
Housing/utilities	_____	_____	_____	_____
Food/liquor/meals out	_____	_____	_____	_____
Furnishings/garden	_____	_____	_____	_____
Clothes	_____	_____	_____	_____
Transportation	_____	_____	_____	_____
Medical/dental	_____	_____	_____	_____
Recreation/travel	_____	_____	_____	_____
Insurance	_____	_____	_____	_____
Gifts/contributions	_____	_____	_____	_____
Income taxes	_____	_____	_____	_____
Personal	_____	_____	_____	_____
Miscellaneous	_____	_____	_____	_____
Savings/investments	_____	_____	_____	_____

expenses as bloated by inflation. To make these calculations check table 2–2 to find the factor for the years before retirement; then multiply each category. You'll soon see why inflation is not as severe as publicized.

Example: If you anticipate that inflation will average 5 percent a year and you have five years to go, use 1.28: for housing $6,000 × 1.28 = $7,680, and so on.

If these future-inflation factored expenses seem horrendous, repeat your calculations at 60 percent. Then, compare your data with the percentages shown in table 3–2. These are national averages and are most useful in pointing out wide variations between what you project and what thousands of families actually spend. You will probably also have to make regional revisions: more for utilities in the cold north; less for recreation if you plan to move to a community/development with a swimming pool and golf course.

Finally, mark increases or decreases in column (3) to keep the total within your projections. You still have time to make the necessary adjustments.

4.   How Much Money You Will Have

This chapter explains the income you will, or can, have after retirement. Some of the data and tables are repetitive—for emphasis and convenience. They are designed to help you to make your own calculations and to show why most people can count on adequate assets after work, if they plan wisely, take advantage of pension plans, save regularly, invest profitably and use common sense. That's what this book is all about.

Sources of Income

For most retirees, there are three sources of assured income: Social Security, pension and savings/investments. Two of these will keep pace, more or less, with inflation: Social Security through annual indexing and savings/investments through high yields and total returns. Pension payments will remain the same except for those who worked for the federal government or a few large corporations.

In discussing how much money you will, and can, have at retirement, I'm using broad figures. As explained in other chapters, the exact amounts will vary, but I believe these projections are, generally, valid.

Note those two words "will" and "can." The opportunities are there. If you do not retire with adequate income, it's probably your own fault. If you earned—or are earning—a reasonable salary/wage, you can set up a pension plan and also save enough to provide for old age. All that's needed is the will and discipline.

It is true, however, that if you have not planned and will retire in the next year or two, there can be trouble ahead. There's not much you can do to enhance after-work income. You can make better use of your assets: by turning nonincome producing property, such as jewelry, collectibles and real estate, into money-making investments. It may be heart-rending to sell the old homestead but if it's worth $100,000 and mortgage free, it represents a potential of $12,000 a year extra income. In most cases, there'll be no tax to pay on the capital gain and even if you use $40,000 to buy or make a down payment on a new home, you'll still have $60,000 to invest. With smaller items, such as jewelry, the proceeds will be less but can still be used for extra income.

The greatest opportunity to boost retirement income is by savings —through an employee savings plan where you work (see box) or with a personal pension plan such as an Individual Retirement Account. For my money, the new IRA, available under the 1981 Economic Recovery Tax Act, is the greatest thing since sliced bread. The annual contribution is deductible from your federal income return (so partially paid by Uncle Sam); the income/appreciation accumulates tax free; and, though the proceeds are taxable when withdrawn, these levies will be modest. *Everyone who has five or more years of work should have an IRA.* That advice goes for both husband and wife when you can afford two plans. A personal pension plan can make the difference between a comfortable and nervous retirement and, to a large extent, can offset the erosion of inflation.

Employee Savings Plan

In theory, this type of plan is hard to beat; in practice, its value depends on the amount of the company's contributions and the tax benefits you receive with an IRA.

With an employee savings plan, the employee contributes a percentage of salary, typically, from 1 percent to 6 percent, with full or partial matching by the employer. The individual's contribution is not tax deductible; that of the company is. Both contributions are invested and their income/appreciation compounds tax free until withdrawal. In most cases, the employee must stay with the company for several years before he is entitled to the corporate contributions. At retirement, however, he gets all of the money, pays a tax only on the employer contributions, and, if he opts for a lump-sum payout, can use the favorable ten-year averaging for his taxes.

Table 4–1 shows the advantages of the extra contributions and tax-free compounding for an employee who earns $20,000 a year, contributes 6 percent ($1,200 a year) with the company matching 50 percent ($600), gets an 8 percent yield on the investment and pays taxes at a 25 percent rate. In twenty years, the dual contribution plan will total $85,665 compared to $45,465 for private savings.

To be sure you are getting the best deal, compare the plan with your own IRA. Here, you can contribute up to $2,000 ($2,250 with nonworking spouse). Since this is tax deductible, it may drop you into a lower bracket. An IRA might be better when the company's matching plan is small, and you expect to move to another job. You always own all of the IRA money.

On the other hand, if you plan to stay with the same company and can look forward to a higher salary, the savings plan will probably be better. Besides, it's a forced savings program and, after you adjust your budget, you'll be happy knowing that you have "hidden" assets ready for your retirement.

To a large extent, the same advice applies to savings/investments. At retirement, all of these assets should be working at maximum rates of return and should be so structured that capital can be withdrawn quickly with no or minimal penalties.

What You Can Have

The majority of people who will retire in the future should have no financial problems, certainly at the outset and, probably, as long as they live. A couple, both aged 65, who will quit work in 1983 can look forward to assured income of as much as $20,000 a year. This is a ballpark figure but, research shows, is justifiable for families with annual working incomes of over $20,000 (as I assume most readers do or will have).

When one partner is younger, or over-the-years income has been

Table 4–1.   Employee Savings Plan Versus Private Savings Account

Employee, earning $20,000, contributes 6 percent of salary to plan: $1,200 a year. Employer matches 50 percent of this: $600 annually. Average yield: 8 percent; tax bracket: 25 percent. All income compounds tax free. After retirement, only the employer contribution portion is taxable (because this was tax deductible when made). If taken in a lump sum, can use ten-year averaging.

After Years	Accumulated Amount	
	Company Savings Plan	Private Savings
10	$ 27,120	$16,290
20	85,665	45,465
30	212,065	97,715

Source: Kwasha Lipton, Consulting Actuaries, Englewood Cliffs, N.J.

relatively low or there is no private pension plan, the income will be less . . . but not much. In such situations, they will be able to get along on a smaller budget and, probably, be willing to work part-time.

Before you disagree with this assertion, do your homework and make your calculations on the basis of full utilization of all of your assets. Most people are worth more than they think. The problem is that they do not always make the most rewarding use of what they own.

The outlook is brighter for those who retire five or ten years hence because these people can assure additional income from personal pension plans.

Here's why:

Retirement Income Projections
for Couples, Both Aged 65, Who Quit Work in

	1983	1988	1993
Social Security	$11,400	$14,600	$18,600
Private pension	3,800	4,000	4,800
Personal pension (IRA)		1,700	4,700
Savings/investments	4,800	3,700	3,900
Total income	$20,000	$24,000	$32,000

Social Security

These figures are rounded out to reflect a 5 percent annual increase by indexing the $10,872 received by the couple who retire in 1982. Based on past raises, which have been as much as 11 percent a year, the actual income will probably be higher. They will, of course, be lower if one partner is under age 65, but they will be higher if the primary wage earner does not retire until after age 65.

Private Pension

The figure $3,800 is a consensus of data involving private and government retirement plans. According to the President's Commission on Pension Policy, 48.1 percent of all active workers are presently covered by some type of employment-based pension, profit-sharing or other retirement plan. But research shows that the higher the individual's earnings, the greater the likelihood of pension coverage. At the income level of those for whom this book was written, my guess is that some 70 percent are protected by pensions.

To be on the safe side the average private pension is set at $3,800 a year. With large, established corporations, governments and the military, the pensions will be greater. For those who were unwilling, or unable to build full vesting, the payout will be lower. For those enrolled in a Keogh Plan or in a pension/profit-sharing plan of a Professional Corporation, the benefits will be much higher.

Accurate data are hard to find. Most of the statistics are out of date, concentrate on large companies and, in many cases, report after-work payments as a combination of private pension and Social Security. To project your own figures, check with your employee relations department or the plan's actuary.

Personal Pension Plan (IRA)

This is *the* greatest opportunity to assure adequate retirement income. It is available to everyone who earns $2,000 a year even though he/she is already a participant in another pension plan.

Since the new rules took effect in January 1982, these benefits are not included until 1988. In those five years, the annual contributions of $2,000 will compound, at 12 percent yield, to $14,240. If you start withdrawing only the annual income at age 65, you will have $1,700 a year—more if you invade capital.

In ten years, your $20,000 savings, again at 12 percent, will be worth $39,300, which can yield $4,700 as long as you both live. Again, the income can be greater—up to $6,000 or so—if you deplete capital.

N.B. I realize that, with some IRAs, the payout will be as an annuity, so that the annual income may be less than 12 percent (see chapter 6). But you can still count on that 12 percent return for eighteen years, longer than the actuarial life of a 65-year-old male and just about that of his same-age spouse.

Investments

This $4,800 a year represents a modest 10 percent return on $48,000. This figure is in line with the conclusions of James H. Schulze in his study, *Income Distribution of Aging.* He states that income from savings amount to 18 percent of retirement income. Since this survey was made when interest rates were about half what they are today, a higher figure seems justified, especially when the couple makes wise use of all assets such as the equity in their home.

If you are not able, or willing, to put all of your wealth to work, you'll have less money and will have to decide to live on less or keep working. The $4,800 is a "can" figure. For those who retire later, in 1988 or thereafter, this category declines because, presumably, more savings will go into an IRA.

Inflation

As noted previously, (1) with proper planning, retirees should not have to make major expenditures for many years and can live within their assured income; (2) inflation is not as severe as headlined (a realistic rate, at this time, is 5 percent a year which is not likely to be more, and may be less, in the future; (3) the longer you live, the lower your expenditures . . . unless you are one of the few unfortunates who incur substantial medical bills.

For worriers, table 4–2 shows the future equivalent of $1,000 purchasing power at various ages before retirement and how much you will have to save, at 10 percent or 12 percent yields, to stay even. If you are now 55 years old, you'll need $1,620: a 12 percent annual payout of a nest egg of $13,583, which can be accumulated with $775 a year and a 10 percent yield.

Or if you already have assets, use table 4–3 for your projections. This can also be used to calculate the impact of inflation.

In addition to my previously mentioned optimism about retiring with adequate income, here are some additional reasons to underscore that attitude:

• For most people, the longer they work, the greater will be their earnings and thus the bigger their pension, and, hopefully, their savings.

Table 4–2.   How Much You Need and Need to Save to Have $1,000 Annual Income Equivalent at Age 65   (Inflation at 5 Percent)

Current Age	Inflation Factor	Future Equivalent of $1,000	Need to Save for 12% Annual Payout	Annual Savings at These Yields 10%	12%
45	2.65	$2,650	$22,082	$ 351	$ 274
50	2.08	2,080	17,333	496	415
55	1.63	1,620	13,583	775	691
60	1.28	1,280	10,667	1,590	1,498

NOTE: Thus, if you need the equivalent of $3,000 after-work income and are now age 55, you will need $40,749: 3 x $13,583. To reach this goal, you must save and invest, each year, $775 with a 10% yield; $691 with a 12% rate of return.

SOURCE: C. Colburn Hardy, *Your Money & Your Life,* American Management Association, New York, N.Y., 1982.

Table 4–3.   **Growth Factors: For Investments and Inflation (Fixed Base)**

Years to Retirement	Compounding Factor if Yield (Inflation) is					
	5%	6%	8%	10%	12%	15%
5	1.28	1.34	1.47	1.61	1.76	2.01
7	1.41	1.50	1.71	1.95	2.21	2.66
10	1.63	1.79	2.16	2.59	3.11	4.05
15	2.08	2.40	3.17	4.18	5.47	8.14
20	2.65	3.21	4.66	6.73	9.65	16.37

NOTE: Use this table with a fixed sum: an investment of $10,000, with a yield of 12 percent, will compound to $31,100 in 10 years: $10,000 x 3.11.

Or if you want to project the dollars you will need if inflation averages 5 percent for the next 5 years, you'll need $1,280 for every $1,000 spent today: $1,000 x 1.28. But remember inflation does not affect every expenditure in retirement.

SOURCE: David Thorndike, ed., *Thorndike Encyclodepia of Banking and Financial Tables*, Warren, Gorham & Lamont, Boston, Mass., 1980.

• More and more women have jobs and either are covered by a pension plan or are able to set up their own IRA.

• Fewer people are taking early retirement. Until recently, more than half of all retirees quit work before age 65. With inflation and the uncertain economy, this trend is shifting and, surveys show, more plan to work past 65 and thus will be able to build larger resources.

• Working after retirement. This may not be part of your dream, but if you can earn money doing what you want to do, work can be a joyous plus. And even if you don't like the job you can find, the added income will be welcome and won't cut your Social Security benefits until you earn more than $6,000 a year . . . with no limits after age 70.

Singles May Have Problems

There is one group of retirees for whom such optimism may not be warranted: single persons, especially those who become widows after their husbands quit work.

Individuals who retire on their own know the income they will get from Social Security, savings and pension. In many cases, they will get more than they had before age 65 (or 62 if they opt for early retirement). They can count on: (1) the full-base Social Security, either their own or that of the deceased spouse when higher; (2) their own pension if they have been covered at work; (3) money from the spouse's pension plan; (4) returns from investing the assets of their husband's estate; (5) their own personal pension plan, such as an IRA. The amount will reflect wise planning (see chap. 12).

The real problems can come with those who are widowed after

retirement. Their Social Security will be one-third less than that received by the couple and, too often, the husband's employer-financed pension will be reduced or eliminated. Unfortunately, too many husbands choose a payout from their company plan for their own life only. This does boost the income as long as the husband lives but leaves nothing for the survivor.

One of the most strongly supported recommendations of the White House Conference on Aging was that, with employer-paid pension plans, both husband and wife must sign an agreement to the payout provisions. The income, for as long as both live, will be lower than that paid to the primary wage-earner but there will be greater security. Unless you can be sure of ample after-work income, make certain that the pension will be paid as long as either partner lives. The same advice goes for personal pension plans when paid out as an annuity.

Making Calculations of Retirement Income

To determine the income available after work, use these tables:

1. Start with Social Security (chap. 5).

2. Refer to table 4–3 to find the income from investments: personal or pension plan. This can be used in planning.

Example: You are now 50 years old and have $10,000 in investments or vested pension fund assets. Their yield is 10 percent. In fifteen years, they will grow to $41,800: $10,000 × 4.18.

3. Use table 4–5 to calculate how your future savings can grow. If you start with an IRA and contribute $2,000 a year, you will save $30,000. At a 12 percent rate of return, these savings will compound to $74,560: $2,000 × 37.28.

Table 4–4.   How Annual Contributions Compound When Made at End of Each Year

Years to Retirement	Compounding Factor at These Annual Yields				
	8%	9%	10%	12%	15%
5	5.87	5.98	6.10	6.35	6.74
7	8.02	9.20	9.49	10.09	11.07
10	14.49	15.19	15.94	17.55	20.30
15	27.15	29.36	31.77	37.28	47.58
20	45.76	51.16	57.27	72.05	102.44

NOTE: If you contribute $2,000 a year for 15 years and the money is invested at an average annual yield of 12 percent, you will have $74,560: $2,000 x 37.28.

SOURCE: David Thorndike, ed., *Thorndike Encyclopedia of Banking and Financial Tables,* Warren, Gorham & Lamont, Boston, Mass., 1980.

Table 4–5.   Calculations Involving Invasion of Capital

Annual Yield	Years Capital Will Last			
	15	20	25	Indefinitely
8%	9.2	10.6	11.5	12.5
9	8.8	10.0	10.7	11.1
10	8.4	9.4	10.0	10.0
12	7.6	8.4	8.8	8.3
15	6.7	7.2	7.4	6.7

SOURCE: C. Colburn Hardy, *Safe in Retirement*, Bantam Books, New York, 1980.

4. To guesstimate the annual income you can count on, multiply the total assets, at retirement, by 12 percent if you anticipate that this is the rate of return you can achieve. If the payout is in the form of an annuity, make it 15 percent. As explained later, this percentage will depend on the type of payout you chose, your age and that of your spouse and the terms set by the pension plan or insurance company.

For those who are worried about inflation, table 4–3 provides the data for projecting inflation. If this averages 5 percent over the next ten years, multiply your present income by 1.28. Thus, if you now earn $30,000, you'll need $38,400 to buy the same goods and services . . . in theory.

To cheer up your spouse, turn to table 4–5. This shows what happens when you invade capital and also the capital you'll need for a set income.

Examples: To get the annual income you can draw from your fund for a set number of years, divide the total retirement capital by the appropriate factor. You project that: (1) you will have $200,000 in pension/savings; (2) the average annual yield will be 10 percent; (3) you want the money to last for twenty years.

$200,000 ÷ 9.4 = $21,276 a year

To find the capital needed for a set annual income for a set number of years, multiply the projected income by the factor for the years you select. You want to receive $25,000 a year for twenty-five years and assume an annual investment return of 12 percent:

$25,000 × 8.8 = $220,000

Case History of Savings for Retirement

Wally B., a 45-year-old executive who plans to retire at age 65, has saved $30,000, which is invested to yield 12 percent annually. He starts his own IRA with a $2,000 contribution each year, again at a yield of 12 percent.

The $30,000 will grow to $289,500 ($30,000 × 9.65 growth factor) when taxes are paid from regular income. The $2,000 IRA contribution ($20,000 total) will compound to $144,100 ($2,000 × 72.05). Together, the at-retirement savings will be $433,600.

At this point, Wally has to decide how to arrange the withdrawal. If he takes a lump sum, he will have to pay taxes of about $127,000: roughly, 25 percent on the first $250,000 and 35 percent thereafter. The exact taxes will depend on his income at age 65 and probably can be lower with ten-year income averaging—not available for IRA payouts. This will leave him with a nest egg of $306,500. At that 12 percent yield, he can count on annual retirement income of $36,780 as long as he and his wife live, and there will be a $306,500 inheritance for the children. This is before-tax income and assumes investment in tax-exempt bonds.

Wally can get a higher income if he uses the $433,600 to buy an annuity. At an annual withdrawal rate of 15 percent, there will be $48,800 a year (before taxes) as long as both Wally and wife live. There will be nothing left for the children. If both die before their anticipated life span, there will be a residue for their heirs.

This example is to show you how much money you can have with wise planning, consistent savings and a personal pension plan. But before you conclude that you'll be living better in retirement than while working, take another look at how inflation reduces purchasing power. Theoretically, that $48,800, with annual inflation at 5 percent, will buy only $18,415 in today's items. Practically, I'd advise Wally to try to boost his investments.

Still, with all of these projections, there is one danger—that both or one partner will live well beyond actuarial age. Inflation will irritate after ten years, pinch after fifteen years and be difficult after twenty years. If you or your spouse come from a long-lived family, consider an annuity. You won't leave much, if anything, to your heirs, but you will both have assured income for life.

Table 4–6.   Calculating Retirement Income from Investments/Pension Plan

Wally B., aged 45, plans to retire at age 65. He has $30,000 in investments, sets up an IRA to which he plans to contribute $2,000 a year. He projects an average annual rate of return of 12%.

	Example	Your Own
1. Current value of investments	$30,000	_____
2. Number of years to retirement	20	_____
3. Estimated annual rate of return	12%	_____
4. Growth factor of fixed sum (table 4–3)	9.65	_____
5. Value of assets at retirement (line 1 x line 4)	289,500	_____
6. Annual contributions to IRA	2,000	_____
7. Growth factor of pension plan (table 4–4)	72.05	_____
8. Value of added contributions at 65 (lines 6 x 7)	144,100	_____
9. Total investments at 65 (Line 5 + line 8)	433,600	_____

10. Lump-sum payout: 306,500

after taxes: of 25% on first $250,000	62,500	
of 35% thereafter	64,600	
Total taxes deducted	127,100	

11. Annual retirement income preserving capital
    withdrawal only income at 12% yield*   36,780
12. Annuity for both partners based on 15% annual   48,800
    withdrawal minus taxes of 25%: $65,040 minus
    $16,260**

* The capital will remain for your estate/heirs.

** The actual payment will reflect the age of your spouse. If both die before actuarial life span, there will be a residue for your heirs. If either lives to or longer than actuarial age, there will be nothing for heirs.

SOURCE: Based on examples used in articles/seminars involving author and Howard J. Wiener, Palm Beach, Fla., tax attorney.

5. Social Security: The Solid Base

Social Security is the base on which all retirement income is built. The monthly checks will be welcome and increasingly ample but will never be enough to assure that financially secure retirement.

Despite the predictions of doomsayers, the basic retirement benefits are NOT going to be reduced. There may be revisions in the method of computation, the amount and timing of indexed increases, terms and dates of eligibility and in methods of financing or tax exemption, but the dollars now paid to retirees will not be less. When the United States Senate votes 95 to 0 against reducing benefits, that's about as definite as any political decision can be!

There are problems and inequities under the present system, but solutions and changes are likely to come as the result of the recommendations of the National Commission on Social Security recently appointed by President Ronald Reagan. This chapter explains Social Security in broad terms because of the probability of changes. In almost every case, the data represent the minimum future benefits and assume that in the years ahead the thrust by Congress will be to encourage private and personal pension plans.

Social Security is the greatest, tax-supported bargain in America. On the average, each current retiree gets back $7 for every $1 paid in Social Security taxes. This ratio will drop in the future, but until well after the year 2000, the individual's benefits will continue to be substantially greater than his/her contributions. And, most important, none of this money is taxed. In effect, every $1.00 from Social Security is equal to between $1.30 and $2.00 of earned income.

Defining Social Security

Before getting into details, let's explain what Social Security does and how it works (or is supposed to work).

1. Basically, it is a form of replacement income. Before you receive

a check, you have to suffer a loss: by death, disability or cessation of normal working income.

2. Unlike employer-financed or personal pension plans, the contributions (from taxes on income paid by both the worker and employer) are not invested for your future benefit. Instead, your money is immediately paid out to individuals who have already stopped working.

A few years ago, four workers supported one retiree; today, the ratio is three to one and, in about thirty years, will be two to one . . . unless significant changes are made. That's the main reason for fears about the financial solvency of the entire Social Security system.

3. Originally, Social Security was established to assure older Americans after-work income. But over the years, Congress has added benefits: payments for disability and for the support and education of children of widows and widowers. These payments, now totaling some $25 billion a year, were approved without provision for additional taxes, and while recent legislation cut them back, they still represent a massive drain on available funds.

4. With people living longer, the payments are much greater than anticipated. A male, born in 1910, and thus eligible for benefits in 1975, had a life expectation, at birth, of 48.6 years; one born in 1920, who can start collecting in 1985, could be expected to live 54.4 years; and one who started life in 1930 could count on an actuarial life of 59.7 years. On the average, a retiree gets his contributions back in less than ten years and thus is living on the earnings of others for the rest of his/her life.

Financing

To pay for the expanded coverage, higher benefits and inflation-based increases, Social Security taxes have risen sharply. At the start, in 1936, the tax was 1 percent of the first $3,000 salary/wages. There were no changes until 1951 when the base was raised to $3,600. Since then, both the base and percentage have gone up and in 1982, taxes were paid on all income up to $32,400 and the tax bite was 9.35 percent for self-employed and 6.7 percent for both employer and employee. By 1986, these figures are scheduled to total 14.3 percent with a maximum base of $39,700. That means, an individual who earns that much will pay $5,677 annually . . . a hefty tax by every standard.

Eligibility and Costs

To attain fully insured status, you must be covered for forty quarters. Once you're eligible, you'll get benefits but the payments will depend on your age at retirement and your earnings over the years. For minimum protection you must work ten years, straight or periodically. If you are away from work for five years, you will lose insured status for disability benefits.

If your wife worked before she married and quit to take care of the children and did not have forty quarters of coverage, she can qualify by earning as little as $1,360 a year (in 1982, but higher thereafter). Whether she earns this in one month or one year, through self-employment or part-time work, she will get credit for four quarters at $340. This will keep alive her disability and survivor's benefits.

Retirement Income

At the normal retirement age of 65, the benefits are calculated by a complex formula: (1) based on average earnings in counted years since 1951, a calculation which usually discards the lowest five years of income; (2) indexed upward annually according to recent wage increases —a shift from the former method which took into account increases in both wages and prices.

Starting in 1982, there was a major revision so that new retirees received less money than those who were born a few months earlier. For those who reach age 65 in 1982, here are the retirement benefits:

	Per Month	Per Year	Spouse	Total
Maximum wage earner	$604	$7,248	$3,624	$10,872
Average wage earner	475	5,700	2,850	8,550
Low wage earner	318	3,816	1,908	5,274

Source: Social Security Administration, West Palm Beach, Fla.

These are minimums which will be adjusted upward annually for inflation.

N.B. Before you wonder why your cousin who became 65 in December 1981 receives a bigger check, here are the comparable figures: for the wage earner: $637, $502 and $333 with total incomes, for both man and wife, aged 65: $11,466, $9,036 and $5,994.

For exact information about your benefits, see your local Social Security office.

Early and Late Retirees

For early retirement, the work credit qualification period is thirty-one quarters in 1982, with an additional quarter each year to forty quarters in 1991.

The benefits are less, depending on the number of months you receive payments before you become 65. The reduction amounts to 20 percent at age 62; 13⅓ percent at age 63; and 6⅔ percent at 64.

When you continue to work past age 65, the benefits go up 3 percent a year until age 71; a total of 15 percent more than would have been received at age 65.

Dollarwise, taking early retirement will pay off if you die before age 77. But you will lose some of the benefits of indexing because the annual increases, made on a percentage basis, will be on a lower base.

In every case, the spouse, when age 65, will receive 50 percent of the primary wage earner's benefits. When both partners are working and qualified, the highest benefit, earned by either, becomes the base. But the maximum payout to the other spouse will be 50 percent of the primary benefit.

Disability Benefits

With an eye on retirement, most people overlook the disability benefits that are paid from Social Security funds. At this time, these are paid, after a waiting period of five months, to individuals who, considering age, education and work experience, are unable to engage in any "substantial gainful work which exists in the national economy." They are calculated by formula that considers the number of dependents but cannot be more than 80 percent of average earnings for the past five years. If you have the ill fortune to become disabled, these payments can be welcome. At age 65, they are automatically turned into retirement benefits.

Family Benefits

Social Security also pays benefits to widows with children under age 16; under 22 when attending college. The college benefits are being phased out, will not be paid from May through August, and will be reduced 25 percent a year through September 1984.

Lump-Sum Benefits

When anyone covered by Social Security dies, there's a lump-sum death benefit to a maximum of $255. This is paid only to the deceased worker's spouse or to children eligible for survivor's benefits. There can be no payment to adult children, relatives or funeral home operators.

Earnings Test

After you start collecting Social Security retirement benefits, you can still earn money—up to limits: $4,440 when you are under age 65; $6,000 from age 65 to 70. If you earn more, you lose $1 in benefits for every $2 in earnings above that limit. You can collect benefits in any month in which you earn no more than $500 if you are over 65; $370 if you are under that age. After you reach age 70, you can earn as much as you want without penalty. *Before you take a job after retirement, do your homework.*

Example: Dr. S., aged 68, has ample income from his pension plan and, for easy figuring, receives $7,200 in Social Security. His wife is 66, so the total benefits are $10,800 a year.

He is offered a part-time job at a clinic, some miles away, at $12,000 annually. To determine the net dollars he'll get, he estimates the federal and state income taxes on this extra income will be $2,500. Since he'll be a consultant, he will have to pay a self-employed Social Security tax of $1,122.

In addition, there will be expenses for transportation, clothing and lunches of $1,200. This brings his income to $7,178: $1,178 more than the allowable $6,000 earned income. He will lose $589 in Social Security so his real net income will be $6,589 . . . not much for a year's work.

His decision should be made on the basis of personal satisfaction, not dollars.

N.B. At the White House Conference on Aging, this earnings test was vigorously opposed, but the facts show that this was more an emotional than logical decision: only 6 percent of all benefits were withheld for this reason.

Discrimination

Social Security was not meant to be unfair, but the original provisions did not foresee some of the great changes in employment and lifestyle that have occurred in recent years. Between 1940 and 1981, the number of adult women who were employed rose from 25 percent to 55 percent and divorces, per marriages, jumped to one in three from one in seven. Since the benefits are based on the primary wage earner's contributions and the payments to the spouse are limited to 50 percent of his checks, two-worker families fare poorly.

Example: Two couples who retired in 1980 ended work with annual earnings of $12,000. In family A., where Mr. A. was the only worker, the annual Social Security checks totaled $7,640 a year. In family B., where both partners worked and contributed equally, the retirement benefits were $6,346. This discrepancy will be greater when one partner dies. Then, the survivor's benefit will be $5,093 for the surviving A. and only $3,173 for the surviving B.

There are also other rules that discriminate against singles, primarily women:

• At age 60, a widow can get benefits based on her age and the amount her deceased husband would have been entitled to or was receiving when he died: from 71.5 percent at age 60 to 100 percent at age 65.

• Disabled widows can get reduced benefits as early as age 50, but if they accept those smaller checks between the ages of 50 and 60, they will receive lower benefits at age 65.

• A widow who remarries at age 60 or older will not suffer a penalty for remarriage. She will get her former husband's benefit, or she can take a wife's benefit, based on payments to her new husband if they are greater. *If you're a 59-year-old widow planning to remarry, wait until you are 60!*

• A woman, aged 62 or older, divorced after ten years of marriage, may get benefits when her ex-husband starts collecting Social Security or disability payments.

• A divorcee, 60 or older (50 if disabled), married for ten years or with young children, may be entitled to widow's benefits when her husband dies even if the ex-husband remarries and his new wife gets Social Security benefits.

For full details of these and other payments, ask your Social Security office for a copy of *A Woman's Guide to Social Security* and *What Women Should Know About Social Security*.

Pending Proposals

When the Commission makes its report, Congress will make changes in the rules and methods of financing. But Social Security Commissioner John A. Svahn has stated that he will not consider two proposals "to bail out Social Security: raising taxes and using general revenues." This means that if no additional sources of revenues are mandated, the rate of increase will be lowered or, possibly, eliminated.

Among the proposals already made are these:

- Pension benefits, at age 65, which now total 42 percent of the final year's earnings, will be cut to 39 percent
- Payments for early retirement, at age 62, will be reduced from 80 percent to 55 percent of the normal age 65 benefits
- Retirement age will be raised to 68
- Annual indexing will be deferred from July to October
- Mandatory retirement age will be raised to 70 with an annual 3 percent increase in benefits for those who work after age 65

But remember: *Congress has already voted overwhelmingly not to reduce benefits.*

What to Do When You Get Ready to Retire

One year before your target date, write Social Security Administration, P. O. Box 56, Baltimore, MD 21203, to get a record of your credits. Be sure to include your Social Security number.

Six months before the big day (if you do not already have information from your employer), visit the local Social Security office to ask for a projection of your total after-work benefits.

Three months before your target date, submit to that office proof of age, such as birth certificate, passport or immigration record. This will give you time to locate lost records.

6. The Wonderful World of Pension Plans

Now let's discuss that most important path to a financially secure retirement: pension plans. These are the keys to assuring adequate after-work income to offset the erosion of inflation. Estimates indicate that some 70 percent of all full-time workers are covered by some sort of employer-paid retirement plan and, as the result of the 1981 Economic Recovery Tax Act, everyone who earns income can set up an IRA. If you have not signed up for your own IRA, do so at once. With an early start, anyone can build that supplementary income and, if you start early enough, you can become a pension millionaire (see table 6–1).

Table 6–1.   What It Takes to Be a Pension Millionaire

Rate of Return	Annual Contributions Must Be for		
	20 Years	30 Years	40 Years
8%	$20,235	$8,174	$3,547
10	15,870	5,527	2,054
12	12,390	3,700	1,164
15	8,488	2,002	489

SOURCE: C. Colburn Hardy, *Dun & Bradstreet's Guide to Your Investments*, Harper & Row, New York, 1982.

To reach that goal, with investments yielding 15 percent, all you need is an annual contribution of $2,002 over thirty years; only $489 over forty years. If you use a Keogh Plan or Professional Corporation Plan, the annual contributions can be greater so that you will reach that million dollars much more quickly.

The magic ingredient is compounding—earning income on income by prompt reinvestment of all earnings. To make your own calculations, use table 6–2. With a regular investment of just $100 a year, at a modest 12 percent rate of return, you will have $1,755 in ten years, $7,205 in twenty years and $24,133 in thirty years.

Table 6-2.   The Power of Compounding

A regular investment of $100 per year invested, at the start of the year at:	Will, when compounded annually, grow to the sum shown for the number of years						
	5	10	15	20	25	30	40
8%	$587	$1,449	$2,715	$ 4,576	$ 7,310	$11,328	$ 25,906
10	610	1,594	3,177	5,727	9,835	16,449	44,259
12	635	1,755	3,728	7,205	13,333	24,133	76,709
14	661	1,934	4,384	9,102	18,187	35,679	134,202
15	674	2,030	4,758	10,244	21,279	43,474	177,909
16	688	2,132	5,166	11,538	24,921	53,031	236,076

To get the corresponding total for any annually invested sum (A), multiply the dollar total given above for the interest rate and number of years by $\frac{A}{100}$. Example: You plan to invest $75 per month, $900 per year. What capital sum will that provide after 30 years, at 12% compounded annually? Check the appropriate figures: 12% for 30 years: $24,133 x $\frac{900}{100}$ = $217,197.

To find out how much you must save and invest, divide the dollar goal by the figure at the anticipated yield. For $100,000 in 20 years, at 12%: $100,000 ÷ $7,205 = $1,388 annual contribution to a tax-advantaged pension plan.

SOURCE: C. Colburn Hardy, *Dun & Bradstreet's Guide to Your Investments*, Harper & Row, New York. 1982.

If you are able to contribute $2,000 annually (the maximum for one individual with an IRA), at age 45, you can retire with $144,100. If you cannot start until age 55, you'll still do O.K.: total assets, at age 65, will be $35,100. Assuming that you invest these sums at 12 percent, you can withdraw 15 percent annually for as long as most people can expect to live: for that $144,100: $21,615 annually; for that $35,100: $5,265. (N.B.: These totals differ from some other figures because they are assumed to be made at the end of each year. If the contributions are made in January, the totals will be greater.)

It's true that the million dollars, in 2022, won't buy as much as they do today, but it's still a nice sum to look forward to. In most cases, your pension plan(s) will represent the difference between a joyous and nervous retirement.

Now let's examine the types and potentials of pension plans. Overall, the pension system is a crazy quilt, but it's improving all the time. As a nation, the United States is committed to providing more and better after-work income. In the past decade, there have been significant improvements: broader private and government benefits; new types of tax-advantaged retirement plans and annuities and, most important, the provisions of the Employee Retirement Income Security Act (ERISA) that became effective in 1974. With few exceptions, every working American can have a retirement plan to supplement Social Security.

There are wide variations in the payments of corporate and government pensions but, in 1980, the average retirement income was more than 40 percent of the final working year's compensation, and by 1985 can be expected to be over 60 percent. In other words, you can count on maintaining close to your old lifestyle when you first quit work. But not for long because of inflation!

Those figures are averages: the president of your company may get 90 percent of $100,000, while a clerk, with average annual earnings of $10,000, will get 45 percent including Social Security. The exact payments will depend on years of service, salary/wages, type of pension plan and whether or not Social Security is an integral part of your retirement benefit.

Accurate information is hard to come by because the stated payments usually cover husband and wife for as long as both live. Such annuities are substantially less than would be paid to the working spouse alone and thus represent a lower percentage of working income.

Here's a summary of the approximate pensions now paid:

Military

After twenty years of service 50 percent of pay; after thirty years 75 percent. Payments start immediately and include a semiannual adjustment for the cost of living. The average enlisted person gets his/her first check at age 39, collects for another thirty-three years and, through other employment, gets Social Security benefits.

Federal Civil Service

Currently, 56 percent of the highest three year earnings when aged 55 with thirty years' service. Since most employees work longer, the percentage is greater. There are no Social Security benefits but there are semiannual cost-of-living adjustments so that, in some cases, older retirees receive more than they did while working.

Civilian Municipal Worker

Total retirement pay is about 33 percent higher than that of private corporate employees, usually includes an inflation escalator but does not involve Social Security unless earned in a separate job.

Police and Fire Fighter

Typically, pensions run about 15 percent above those of other city employees, permit early retirement (often after twenty years) and include liberal tax-free disability payments.

Employees of Small Companies

While many are not covered at all, those who do receive pensions get approximately 50 percent of their last working year's compensation plus Social Security.

Employees of Large Corporations

Generally, the total pension plus Social Security will be over 60 percent of last year's income: higher for executives, lower for hourly workers. Only a few pension plans have automatic increases to help offset inflation, but this number is rising steadily.

Checkpoints for Corporate Pension Plan

Whether you are 26 or 62, you should understand your rights and rewards. Get a booklet explaining your pension plan from your employer or your union and, with your spouse, look for answers to questions like these:

• Are there survivor's benefits? Will the pension stop at the death of the wage earner or continue for the surviving partner?

• Will the widow get income if her husband dies before age 55?

• Are all corporate employees covered? One company had a union-negotiated plan for plant workers but nothing for secretaries.

• How are the benefits computed? On final salary/wages? Average of the past five years? Highest three years?

• Will the pension be integrated with Social Security? If so, will the total payment be frozen even if Social Security benefits increase?

• Do you meet (or will you meet) minimum qualifications for maximum benefits? As the result of ERISA, most plans vest participants 25 percent after five years and 100 percent after ten years.

• Can you make voluntary contributions? If so, how much? Will they be matched by your employer?

• What are minimum work requirements? Usually, they are 1,000 hours per year.

• What about breaks-in-service? Can you get credit for past service if you leave for child-birth, education, illness?

• Does the plan cover those who start work after age 45?

• Will there be a built-in cost-of-living increase?

• At what age can you begin to receive full benefits?

• If you retire early, how will your benefits be calculated?

• If you work beyond normal retirement age, how will your pension be increased?

• Will your employer automatically submit your pension application? If not, where should you submit form? What documents should be included?

• If you are denied benefits, where do you file an appeal?

If you do not fully understand any provision or cannot find an answer to any question, ask the industrial relations department for an explanation.

Periodically, and especially when nearing retirement, ask the plan administrator for full details: the anticipated value of your pension for yourself and for your surviving spouse. By law, this information should be readily available . . . in writing. Do not delay getting answers. After all, it is, or will be, your money.

Early Retirement

The idea of quitting work before age 65 is intriguing, but it is seldom financially practical. Most people will not have enough savings to live comfortably for the next twenty years after age 60 (about halfway between the anticipated life spans for both sexes). A few years can make a big difference. At 5 percent inflation, the purchasing power of every $1,000 will be cut to $754 in five years and to $614 in ten years. *But this does not apply fully to all retirement expenses.*

On the other hand, at a 10 percent return, compounded annually, a single $1,000 investment will grow to $1,610 in five years and to $2,594 in a decade.

A much more important consideration, especially for those employed by large organizations, is continuation of protection through group life and health insurance. Both are expensive for individuals to buy in their 60s and Medicare does not start until age 65 (except for disability).

Unless the worker has long years of service, his corporate/government pension, at age 60, will be about one-third less than that at 65: $667 per month instead of $1,000. Social Security does not start until age 62 (except for widows) and then at a 20 percent reduction for the primary beneficiary and 25 percent less for the eligible spouse. Thus, if, at age 65, you are entitled to $600 and your spouse to $300 ($900 total per month), at age 62, you will get 80 percent ($480) and your spouse will get 75 percent ($225) for a total of $705.

At age 63, the factors are .866 and .833, respectively: in dollars, $519.60 and $249.90, for a total of $769.50; at age 64, .933 and .916, or $559.80 and $274.80, for a total of $834.60.

All Social Security benefits are indexed to the cost of living (recently, 14 percent a year) but if you continue to work, your base for the annual increase will be substantially larger and will grow at a more rapid rate. If you take another job, your extra income will still be subject to limitations until you are 72 years old.

Financially, it seldom pays to take early retirement.

Employee Savings Programs

One of the most rewarding types of savings-for-retirement programs is the employee savings program. Your voluntary contributions are matched, partially or fully, by your employer.

There are limits: IRS permits voluntary contributions up to 6 percent of total mandatory employee contributions with a corporate retirement plan; individual companies usually set a maximum of employee income: i.e., 10 percent of the first $20,000 salary/wages.

The corporate contribution is tax deductible by the corporation but all contributions, both corporate and personal, are taxable to the employee. The big plus is that all monies compound tax free until withdrawn. As a result, long-term savings mount up rapidly. As shown by table 6–3, an employee earning $20,000 a year, who makes a voluntary contribution of 6 percent ($1,200) with 50 percent matching by the company ($600), will build a nest egg more than double that which he can accumulate with private savings when the average annual yield is 8 percent. Since the employee uses after-tax dollars, only the employer's contribution is taxable when the savings are withdrawn after retirement (see table 4–1).

This is a terrific deal. If your employer has this type of employee savings program, join it at once and contribute the maximum every year.

Deferred Compensation

If you are an executive of a small or medium-size corporation, one of the best ways to build extra assets for retirement is by means of deferred compensation. (The idea is valid with major companies but, usually, too difficult to administer.) Under such plans, the corporation gets current and future tax deductions and you get added income fifteen or twenty years from now. There are many variations but this example will give you an idea of how such plans work.

Jim C., aged 45, is vice president of a consistently profitable, family-controlled company. A $10,000 raise would be taxed at the 50 percent rate, so Jim arranges for his money to be deferred compensation and invested in shares of a mutual fund.

Using these shares as collateral, the company borrows $4,000 to buy paid-up-at-65 life insurance that will give Jim about $110,000 coverage.

The corporation deducts both the $4,000 and the annual interest. Jim gets extra protection for his family now and owns an ever-more valuable asset. He must pay income tax on the $4,000 premium, but that's a lot less than he would have to pay on a $10,000 raise. He borrows this money against the cash value of the policy and deducts the interest on his income tax return.

Here's what happens as Jim grows older:

Age 45–55: The situation continues each year: the company invests $10,000 for Jim, pays the insurance premium with borrowed money and takes tax deductions; Jim pays income tax on the premium with a loan against the policy.

Age 55–65: By this time, the investment fund is yielding enough to pay for the $10,000 deferred compensation so the company can stop this annual payment *if* it wants to do so. But it keeps borrowing the $4,000 premium and takes its tax deductions. Jim continues to borrow to pay the extra taxes.

Age 65–75: At retirement:

- Jim owns the paid-up policy. He can keep it and let its cash value increase or he can cash it in, pay off the outstanding loans and invest the balance.

- The company sells some of the fund shares to get money to pay off its loans and repay itself for all taxes (income and capital gains) paid over the twenty years.

- The balance of the fund (which continues to earn income), is paid out to Jim over ten years: at a rate of $15,000 to $20,000 annually depending on fund performance. The company deducts these payments as business expenses.

Result: Jim defers $10,000 a year while working to get $15,000 or more annually for ten years after retirement. The company cost is little or nothing because of the tax benefits.

For Employees of Nonprofit Institutions

Special pension plans are available for people who work for nonprofit institutions such as hospitals, social service agencies and foundations. They are allowed to set aside 20 percent of their salary with the same advantages of other qualified retirement plans: tax deduction of the contribution and no tax on income/appreciation until withdrawn.

These plans are open to employees paid a regular salary. They are nonforfeitable after one year. The institution can make direct contributions or the employee can agree to take a lower salary and have the difference invested in the retirement plan.

The savings are invested in a trusteed fund, usually managed by an insurance company. Taxwise, this is a good deal; from the investment viewpoint, it's marginal because part of the money is used to buy life insurance and the rates of return on the balance are seldom sensational.

This is another illustration of how government/society sets up programs that encourage retirement planning.

Personal Pension Plans

There are three kinds of personal pension plans: Individual Retirement Account (IRA); Keogh Plan (HR–10); and Professional Corporation. All must be qualified by IRS and have a trustee, usually a financial institution. Administration, including investing, can be self-directed or assigned. If you turn over management to someone else, you will have to pay fees but all you have to do is to sign the annual reports.

You can be the manager and handle the investments through a stockbroker or agent with the assets held by a custodian. When there are participating employees, the employer is legally responsible for all operations including prudent investments.

Fees for pension plans range from zero with thrift institutions to $30 a year for mutual funds for single retirement plans; to about $75 plus $3 per transaction for banks; to $250 and/or 0.2 percent of total assets for large portfolios such as those of professional corporations.

Under the Economic Tax Recovery Act of 1981 the most significant changes in retirement plans involved IRAs. There are three types: straight, Simplified Employees Pension (SEP) and IRA Rollover.

With all three, withdrawals are permissible at age 59½ and mandatory at 70½. The proceeds can be taken out in a lump sum, directly or with income averaging or as an annuity.

Early withdrawals are subject to a penalty of 10 percent of the takeout (but that's cheaper than the cost of a loan), are taxable as ordinary income and are not eligible for income averaging when the payment is made in a lump sum. These restrictions do not apply to early death or disability.

Straight IRA

Under the new law, anyone, even though enrolled in a pension plan other than a straight IRA, can set up his/her own IRA with earned income. The maximum annual contribution is $2,000 ($2,250 with a nonworking spouse). This is fully deductible on the participant's federal income tax return in the year of allocation.

If you are a professional or own your business, you can put your spouse on the payroll at $2,124 and pay a tax-deductible $2,000 to her IRA and $134 for Social Security. And if your children earn money from delivering papers or mowing lawns, a grandparent (who is not responsible for their expenses) can contribute to their IRA the sum of their total earnings up to $2,000 a year. When the child can afford to make his/her own contributions, he/she can take over. At 65, with wise investments, there will be over $1 million!

Simplified Employees Pension (SEP)

With this, the contributions are made by the company to the lesser of 15 percent of earned income or $7,500. It's a handy way for a small organization to set up retirement income because the contributions are tax deductible.

IRA Rollover

This is sort of a supplementary pension plan that can be used with lump-sum distributions from any type of pension plan. It's a tax-free transfer of savings for those who quit one job early. The money must go directly to the new IRA. If you deposit any money from the payout in your personal account, you must pay taxes at the regular income tax rate.

A rollover is wise under two conditions:

1. On leaving the employ of one company while waiting for qualification under a new pension plan. Thus, if Mary moves from New York to Florida, she can take her share of the pension plan and roll it over into an IRA. There can be no distribution until she is 59½. But she can enroll in a new pension plan at her new job.

2. When you take early retirement and receive a substantial lump sum from a pension plan.

Example: Stu S., aged 55, has worked for a corporation for twenty-seven years. In the last five years, his earnings have averaged $49,000 annually. Under the distribution formula, he will get $14,156 a year: a total of $325,588 if he lives his actuarial twenty-three years.

Stu opts for a lump-sum payment. This is $104,237 based on a 12¼ percent interest rate. He rolls this over into an IRA and invests the money at a 12 percent yield.

At age 60, Stu withdraws $14,156 annually for ten years. At age 70½, IRS requires that the payouts be increased to draw down the assets to zero at his new actuarial age of 81. His savings continue to compound so that, in the last year, he must take out $84,736. With an IRA rollover, he receives $778,422 between ages 60 and 81. This is more than double what he would have received from a regular pension between the ages of 56 and 81.

Distribution of IRAs

Since the contributor always owns all of the assets of the IRA, he can choose the method of payment. But since the contributions were tax deductible, all proceeds are taxable at the then current income tax rate.

These are the options:

• Lump-sum payment. You pay the tax and can spend or invest the balance. This is best for modest savings. Or you can income average (chap. 7). This is best for substantial sums. In all cases, check with your tax adviser first.

• Life annuity. Withdrawals are made according to the life expectancy of *both* partners. Thus, if your wife is three years younger, she will have a life expectancy of about twenty years when you retire, so the payouts can be made over two decades. In the meantime, the remaining capital accumulates earnings tax free. This slow takeout can be VERY profitable.

Example (based on *Forbes* data): Bob A. contributes $2,250 into an IRA for twenty-five years: a total of $56,250. Being very conservative, he invests at a 10 percent rate of return. When he retires at age 70, the pension fund is worth $243,409.

In year 1, the nest egg will earn $24,893 (full year of compounding). With a withdrawal of $12,850, the net cash value of the fund rises to $255,452. Even in retirement, he is boosting his assets.

By year 5, the earnings will be $29,483 and the takeout $19,139 so the net cash value will be $300,362. In year 10, things begin to even out: the income is $32,894 and the outgo, $31,489, and the assets total $329,459.

From then on, the outgo is greater than the earnings so that, by year 20, the earnings are down to $4,509 but the payout, to clear out the account, is a whopping $85,242. Over forty years (twenty contributing; twenty taking out), Bob saved $56,250 and, theoretically, can take out $776,573. That is one SURE way to beat inflation.

Death Payments

In most cases, if death occurs before the fund is depleted, the remainder goes to the heirs. When installment payouts are selected, the terms are based on the life expectancy of the beneficiary/beneficiaries, according to IRS tables. When the beneficiary is someone other than your estate, the payout is tax free when the beneficiary draws the money out over the lesser of life or thirty-six months.

How an IRA Can Cost Less Than $1 Per Day

When both husband and wife are working, an IRA can be a real tax/money saver. Let's say that Stu and Anne earn $30,000: Stu, $20,000 as a teacher, Anne, $10,000 as a secretary. With normal deductions/exemptions, they are in the 33 percent tax bracket so, in 1982, pay $9,900 in federal income taxes.

Stu sets up an IRA with $2,000 so the family's taxable income drops to $28,000. In addition, there's a 5 percent deduction of the earned income of the lower-paid spouse: a maximum of $1,500 in 1982, but 10 percent to a maximum of $3,000 in 1983. With this $500, their tax base falls to $27,500 so their rate is 29 percent and their tax is $7,975, a "savings" of $1,925. In effect, the pension costs only $75 a year! To be on the safe side, let's say that the cost is $1 per day for a pension plan that can provide as much as $1 an hour in retirement.

Better yet, with lower taxes and greater deductions in future years, the "cost" of an IRA will be even less. In 1983, with the same income, Stu and Anne will be in the 26 percent tax bracket. No wonder most knowledgeable people feel that IRAs are the greatest thing since sliced bread.

Keogh Plan

This is the oldest personal pension plan. It dates back to 1962 when the maximum contribution was the lesser of $2,500 or 10 percent of earned income. Since then, the limits have been raised so that, under the 1981 Economic Tax Recovery Act, the maximum standard contribution is 15 percent of earned income up to $15,000 a year. But, as we'll see, it is possible to contribute more under a Maxi-Keogh. And if inflation continues, chances are there will be higher limits in the years ahead.

Keogh Plans are widely used by small business organizations and professionals such as physicians, dentists, architects, etc. As with all qualified retirement plans, all contributions are deductible on federal income tax returns and all income and appreciation on the plan's assets accumulate tax free until withdrawn, permissable at age 59½ and mandatory at 70½.

Eligibility

All employees are eligible for participation as soon as they are hired and must be included when they have completed three years of service —defined as a twelve-month period in which the employee has worked one thousand hours.

Vesting

Once the employee becomes eligible, all his/her contributions are vested immediately. These benefits may be paid at death or disability, can be paid on termination of employment or deferred but not later than the retirement date specified in the written plan, usually at age 65.

Contributions

These are made solely by the employer who is not permitted to reduce the regular compensation paid to a participant to offset the earnings. Under certain conditions, the plan may be integrated with Social Security. The annual contribution, as a percentage of earned income, must be the same for everyone.

Types of Plans

These are the types of Keogh Plans:

Defined Contribution (money purchase) (DCP)

With this, the annual contribution is a fixed portion of salary to a maximum of 15 percent (20 percent in 1984).

Example: If Dr. H. sets aside 15 percent of his $80,000 income

($12,000), he must contribute $3,000 for his office manager who earns $20,000.

Profit-sharing

This is similar to a DCP but contributions are based on a fixed percentage of profits. This cannot exceed 15 percent of earned income or $15,000.

Example: If Dr. H. should earn $120,000, his maximum contribution would be $15,000 even though 15 percent of $120,000 is $18,000. But since $15,000 is 12.5 percent of income, he could reduce the contributions for employees to the same percentage: $2,500 for the office manager.

Defined Benefits (DBP)

Under this type of plan, you start with the projected retirement income, determine the assets needed to furnish such an amount and then contribute the money needed to compound to that sum at retirement: at age 65 or at age 70 if the participant has been in the plan for five years. These projections are made by IRS rules. For a male, aged 50, earning $80,000 a year and planning to quit work at age 65: $80,000 $\times$ .03 $\times$ 15 = $36,000 annual retirement benefit (see table 6–3).

That $36,000 base annuity requires a total accumulation of $338,400. To build that nest egg in fifteen years, the annual contributions would start at $13,717, assuming a 6 percent rate of return. That means that Dr. H. can shelter $1,217 more than the $12,000 a year with a regular

Table 6–3.   How To Calculate Defined Benefit Under Keogh Plan

C x SP x YFP = ARB		
	C	= Current Compensation
	SP	= Statutory Percentage
	YFP	= Years of Future Participation
	ARB	= Annual Retirement Benefit

IRS Statutory Percentages	
Starting Age	Multiplying Factor
30 or less	6.5
35	5.4
40	4.4
45	3.6
50	3.0
55	2.5
60 or over	2.0

SOURCE: Research & Review Service of America, *The Keogh Manual,* Indianapolis, Ind., 1982.

Keogh. If the yields of investments are higher than 6 percent, the future contributions must be reduced or IRS will assess penalties.

The same formula is used with contributions for employees.

Withdrawals/Benefits

With a DBP, the money cannot be taken out in a lump sum but must be in the form of an annuity. If the participant dies before age 65, the surviving spouse will get the assets in the pension fund and no extra death benefit.

In the retirement income, Dr. H. has these choices:

Straight Annuity

This provides $36,000 a year for life with nothing for his widow if he dies before the assets are paid out. Actuarially, he should live to age 79. If he lives longer, he will still get $36,000 annually.

Annuity with Life Insurance

Here, the annual payout is 91 percent, or $32,760 a year, but there will be cash for his widow. The amount will depend on his lifespan.

Joint Survivor

There is income as long as either partner lives. Payments will be reduced by 25 percent so Dr. H. would get $27,000 for life and his widow would be sure of $23,962 as long as she lives.

With a DCP or profit-sharing plan, the assets can be taken out in a lump sum and invested as you see fit. The income will not be guaranteed and may be less than that of an annuity but, unless you speculate and lose money, there will be an inheritance for your children.

Family Bonus

A DBP plan makes it possible to boost your family's after-work income by putting your wife on the payroll. She must be a genuine employee for at least ten years. Here's how this can be done:

Mrs. G. is 45 years old and no longer has to stay home to care for the children. Her husband hires her at a modest salary of, say, $5,000 a year. This is not likely to be attacked by IRS.

Under a DBP, her after-work pension is set at $5,000 a year. This will require assets of $36,000 at that 6 percent yield. To achieve that goal, the annual contribution, for her benefits, will be $571 a year—tax deductible.

Voluntary Contributions

Under the new law, any participant may make an annual voluntary contribution of 10 percent of earned income to a maximum of $2,500. When this is made by an employee, $2,000 is tax deductible. But if the plan covers only owner-employers, voluntary contributions are not permitted but the boss(es) can establish an IRA to secure the extra tax benefits.

These are rather detailed explanations to point out the versatility and scope of personal pension plans. Many of these provisions are complex and subject to IRS regulations, so before you set up a special pension, check with a knowledgeable attorney, actuary and, when substantial sums are involved, investment adviser.

Professional Corporation Pension Plans

For those with relatively high incomes, these are the most rewarding pension plans. They permit the largest tax-deductible contributions (and thus the highest, after-work income), the greatest flexibility and the most tax savings. Under a properly structured plan, Uncle Sam will pay as much as half of the cost of contributions for an employee in the 50 percent tax bracket.

Professional corporations are expensive to establish and administer and require payment of Social Security taxes for all employees, so, generally, are best for those with annual incomes of $75,000 or more. In most cases, these added costs will be offset by: (1) the corporation's lower tax bracket, the ability to shelter more income through higher, after-tax returns on investments; (2) the fringe benefits, such as corporate payments of health, life and disability insurance premiums and medical expenses.

Types of Pension Plans

With corporations, there can be a wide choice of retirement plans with high contributions and after-work benefits—adjusted annually for inflation in the future.

Contributions are made by the corporation and are tax deductible as business expenses. But you can also make voluntary contributions up to 10 percent of your annual compensation. These savings accumulate tax free until withdrawn. Here are the choices:

Defined Contribution Plan (DCP)

This calls for a set annual allocation up to 25 percent of compensation to a maximum annual amount that is adjusted each year for inflation. Currently, this is $30,000 per participant. Revisions in basic plans must be approved by IRS and can be subject to penalties.

With DCPs, these are the options:

• *Money purchase:* a fixed percentage of annual salary applies to each employee. The maximum contribution is 25 percent of annual compensation with a current limit of $30,000 per participant.

• *Profit-sharing:* the set-aside varies annually with corporate profits. The maximum contribution is 15 percent of total individual compensation.

• *Combined money purchase and profit-sharing:* on a percentage basis, the contributions must be the same for all employees. The maximum, per participant, is the lesser of 25 percent of compensation or $30,000 a year.

Defined Benefits Plan (DBP)

This is the most attractive option with corporate plans. The annual contribution is based on the desired retirement income and the number of years you work before the stated retirement age, usually 65, but earlier or later if so stated in the plan provisions.

You start with the after-work dollars per year you want, determine the assets needed to furnish such a benefit and then set the corporate contribution at the amount needed to compound to that goal. As with a Keogh Plan, the projections are made by IRS tables and contributions must be lowered if the assets grow at a faster-than-anticipated rate.

The ultimate annual benefit is limited to 100 percent of your average annual compensation for the five highest, consecutive years of employment, with a maximum of $90,000, also adjustable upward for inflation after 1985. Roughly, this will require assets of $1.3 million.

A variation of this is the *Target Benefit Plan.* The goal is set by formula and the annual dollar contributions remain basically the same over the years regardless of investment gains or losses.

There can also be combination plans which, generally, follow the same requirements/projections/limitations (see table 6–4).

Table 6–4(a).   Requirements/Benefits of Pension and Profit-Sharing Plans: IRA and Keogh Plan

	Individual Retirement Account (IRA)	Keogh Plan Defined Contribution (DCP)	Defined Benefit (DCB)
Contributions	$2,000 single; $2,250 with nonworking spouse but not more than annual earned income: up to $7,500 when paid by employer	15% of compensation to $15,000 a year on basis of $100,000 earnings. On income above this, to $200,000, 7.5% to maximum of $15,000*	Based on IRS tables; can be more than DCP depending on age and years paid.
Vesting	Immediate	Immediate for eligible employees as set by plan, but must include all with 3 years' service of 1,000 hours per year	Same as DCP
When employee leaves	Always owns all	Takes entire amount	
Investment earnings/losses	Retained in fund until withdrawn; permissible at 59½; mandatory at 70½	Added to or subtracted from account balance	Annual contribution adjusted to reflect gains or losses by actuary under IRS rules
At retirement, recipient gets	Lump sum, annuity or annual payout keyed to life expectancy of younger partner	Balance of account as lump sum, annuity or long payout (see IRA).	Predetermined amount based on age at start under IRS tables: total benefits limited

* In 1984, maximum of $30,000 and 20% of compensation.

Table 6-4(b). Requirements/Benefits of Pension and Profit-sharing Plans: Professional Corporation Defined Benefits Plan

	Fixed Benefit	Target Benefit	Combination Plan	
			Money Purchase	Fixed Benefit
Contributions	Amount needed to fund predetermined benefit	Amount needed to fund predetermined benefit by maximum of 25% of compensation to $30,000	To 10% of compensation as fixed in advance	Amount needed to fund predetermined benefit up to 100% of compensation, not to exceed $90,000 annually*
Vesting	As set by corporation plan but can be amended			
When employee leaves	Corporate contributions cut by amount of forfeited funds			
Investment gains/losses	Annual contribution adjusted to reflect gains/losses	Added to or subtracted from account balance		Annual contribution adjusted to reflect gains/losses
At retirement, participant gets	Predetermined amount to 100% compensation to maximum of $90,000*	Benefits determined by applying formula to compensation; depends on growth of fund assets. Contribution based on actuarial assumptions but cannot exceed 25% of compensation to maximum of $30,000*	Balance of account	Predetermined amount to 100% of compensation to maximum of $90,000*

* Adjusted annually for inflation after 1985.

Table 6–4(c).   Requirements/Benefits of Pension and Profit-sharing Plans: Professional Corporation Defined Contribution Plan

	Money Purchase	Profit-Sharing	Combination Money Purchase and Profit-sharing
Contributions	Up to 25% of compensation to maximum of $30,000 annually, fixed in advance	Varies annually, up to 15% of compensation to maximum of $30,000	To 25% of compensation (part fixed, part variable) to maximum of $30,000
Vesting	As set by corporation: typically, after 4 years: 40% with additional 10% annually for next 6 years; after 10 years: 100%.		
When employee leaves	Corporate contributions cut by amount of forfeited funds	Forfeited funds added to remaining account balance of participants	Forfeited funds reduce corporate contributions in pension plan; added to account balance in profit-sharing
Investment earnings/losses	Added to or subtracted from account balance		
At retirement, participant gets	Balance of account in lump sum, annuity when funds commingled		

SOURCE: Internal Revenue Service, Jacksonville, Fla.

How to Contribute More Than 100 Percent of Salary

To give you an idea of the flexibility of Professional Corporation Plans, here's an example of how a physician contributed more than his total salary for his personal retirement benefits. It combines a DBP and DCP so that the corporation can make maximum allocations based on the number of years to retirement.

Example: Dr. F. is 45 years old and in ten years wants to quit his practice to teach. His net income is $160,500, which he can take out in salary, bonus and pension contributions. With only his wife to support, he feels he can live comfortably on $75,000 a year. Thus, he can make an annual contribution of $85,500 for his after-practice benefits. Here's how:

The Professional Corporation sets up a DBP to fund a retirement benefit of 100 percent of his $75,000 salary. That income will require $1,025,000, which, in turn, requires an annual allocation of $78,000.

At age 55, Dr. F. can withdraw the money, roll it over, tax free, into an IRA, and be sure of over $75,000 a year as long as both he and his wife live. Or he can take out part of the savings and start a final withdrawal at age 70½.

That's not all, says Howard J. Wiener, Palm Beach, Florida, tax attorney. Dr. F. can get an additional $35,000 a year by setting up a 10 percent DCP under the 1.4 rule. The 1 represents the 100 percent of compensation benefit per year under the DBP. The 0.4 is 40 percent of the maximum allowable contribution of 25 percent of compensation under the DCP. Thus, the extra allocation, made by the corporation, is 10 percent of $75,000 or $7,500 a year. Together with the $78,000, this means a total annual contribution of $85,500.

In ten years, when Dr. F. wants to start teaching, this $7,500 a year, compounded at 10 percent, will grow to $131,475 and, with no further contributions, will be worth $140,520 when he's 65 years old. This will provide an annuity of over $35,000 a year. Dr. F. can count on afterwork income of at least $110,000 which, despite inflation, should be ample for a financially secure and carefree retirement.

Vesting

Employees of corporations, whether professional or business firms, "own" their share of pension plans according to terms set by the original standards under the Employee Retirement Income Security Act (ERISA):

- Cliff vesting: fully vested after ten years of service
- Graded vesting: 25 percent after five years' service, five percent for each additional year up to ten years plus an additional 10 percent for each year thereafter, so 100 percent vested in fifteen years
- Rule of 45 vesting: 50 percent vesting for employees with five years' service when age and years of service add up to 45 plus 10 percent for each additional year up to five years.

Keep these in mind when you are considering leaving your job. It is possible that if you stayed on another few months, you could look forward to a pension. Chances are that it won't be paid until you're 65, but it could be a welcome addition to your income.

Further Comments

The impact of timing. The earlier you start saving and investing, the wealthier you will be. Refer to table 6–2 to see why. In the first five years, with a 10% yield, the $100 annual investments ($500) grow to $610; in ten years, the $1,000 savings mount to $1,594; in twenty years, the $2,000 contributions are worth $5,727; and, in thirty years, the $3,000 savings soar to $16,449.

The importance of higher yields. In ten years that $100 a year, compounded at 12 percent, grows to $1,755; at 14 percent, to $1,934. In twenty years, the comparable figures are $7,205 and $9,102; and in thirty years, the higher returns build assets half again as great: $35,679 compared to $24,133.

To calculate how much you must save each year to reach your goal. Use tables 6–2 and 6–5. If you are now 45 years old, plan to retire in twenty years and feel you need annual retirement income, in today's dollars of $12,000, you will need a nest egg of $240,000. (This is only a 5 percent yield so, in effect, you assume that a 12 percent yield will more or less offset inflation.)

If you have $160,000 in your pension plan (this could include savings/ investments but their income is taxable so the calculations will be more difficult), you will have to save $5,333 annually. This is 17.7 percent of your current $30,000 salary. It won't be easy but, hopefully, you will get raises to make such savings possible. And taxes will be lower in the future.

High taxes on retirement income. Do not be fooled by advertise-

Table 6–5. Are You Saving Enough?

1. Annual retirement income desired, in today's dollars, not counting Social Security	$12,000
2. Years of life expectancy after 65	20
3. Nest egg required (line 2 x line 1)	$240,000
4. Present nest egg	$160,000
5. Additional capital needed (line 3 — line 4)	$80,000
6. Years to retirement	15
7. Annual savings needed, in today's dollars (line 5 ÷ line 6)	$5,333
8. Current annual income	$30,000
9. Percent to save each year (line 7 ÷ line 8)	17.7%

ments of thrift institutions and insurance companies that stress that you will be taking your retirement income when you are paying taxes at a lower rate. This will not be true for many high-income executives and professionals. If inflation continues at a modest rate, you may be paying taxes at a rate that is as high as you are paying while working.

Example: Mike J., aged 34, earns $30,000 and is in the 30 percent tax bracket. If his salary rises at an annual rate of 8 percent, he will be making over $300,000 at retirement. At half his last working year's income, he'll retire with $150,000 annually. This sounds tremendous but he will be in the 50 percent tax bracket so may end up with $75,000.

Personal pension plans can be the key to a comfortable, secure retirement. If you work for a corporation which permits you to make contributions, do so, especially if they are fully or partially matched by the company. If you are enrolled in a Keogh Plan or Professional Corporation, find out about Defined Benefit Plans that permit larger contributions. And, in almost all cases, consider setting up your own IRA. With personal pension plans, the contributions are tax deductible so will lower your tax bracket. And, most important, your savings will compound tax free. A personal pension plan is one sure way to beat inflation.

7. Tax Breaks

When you reach age 65, there are extra exemptions, benefits and deductions on your federal income tax return so that, generally speaking, no taxes need be paid until your income is over $20,000 a year. There are no levies on Social Security and Railroad Retirement Benefits, and with proper planning, there can be tax savings on your pension whether taken as a lump sum or annuity.

To get full, up-to-date information, ask your local IRS office for a copy of *Tax Benefits for Older Americans.* For data on state taxes, write to American Association of Retired Persons, 1909 K Street, N.W., Washington, D.C. 20049, for a free copy of *State Tax Facts.*

Here's a summary of the most important savings in retirement with the federal tax when you are 65 years or older.

- You get double personal exemptions: $2,000 for an individual; $4,000 for husband and wife with joint filing.
- You do not have to pay a tax (but may have to file an annual return) when income is over $4,300 for a single taxpayer; $5,400 for a surviving spouse over 65; $6,400 for joint return when one spouse is over 65; $7,400 when a married couple, with joint return, are both 65 or older.
- There's also a Tax Credit for the Elderly. This applies primarily to those with low incomes.
- There is a credit for Care of Certain Dependents. This is specifically defined as costs of household services and expenses of the disabled dependent which are incurred in order to permit the taxpayer to be gainfully employed: a maximum of $2,400 for one dependent; $4,800 for more than one—plus credits of 30 percent of qualified expenses when gross income is $10,000 or less; a reduction of 1 percent for each additional $2,000 income up to $28,000 and a maximum of 20 percent thereafter. Finally, for nursing/aged home care, the entire cost of maintenance is a deductible medical expense on the regular 1040 form.

Taxes on Pension Income

With a pension or annuity, the tax status depends on whether the retiree contributed to the cost of the benefit.

The full amount, whether taken in a lump sum or as an annuity, is taxable if: (1) the employer paid everything; (2) you made all the contributions, such as to a personal pension plan (these contributions were tax deductible when made).

But if you and your employer both made contributions, there's no tax if you recover your contribution within three years. Thereafter, all receipts must be reported in your gross income.

Basically, there are no taxes on the amount of the payout that represents return of capital. This is determined by IRS formulas related to life expectancy. To illustrate this concept and avoid the complications that come with preretirement contributions, let's take the case of a retiree who purchases an annuity with her own savings.

Example: Joan S., aged 75, buys a nonrefund annuity for $10,000. She will receive $100.62 per month as long as she lives. Since her life expectancy is twelve years, IRS regulations permit $69.44 to be tax exempt as a return of capital. The balance is taxable income.

The expected return from the contract is $14,489.28: 144 months x $100.62. Since her cost was $10,000, the interest portion, $4,489.28, is taxable.

Tax Savings with Pensions

There are several options on taxation of pension fund lump-sum distributions. Let's say that, after retirement, you will be in the 25 percent tax bracket and that you are due to receive $58,000.

- If you roll over the money into an annuity, you will get about $7,000 annually, fully taxable each year.
- If you take it in cash, you will pay Uncle Sam about $14,500 and have $43,500 to invest. Each year, you will pay taxes on the income at your then current tax rate.
- Ten-year averaging. To be eligible for these savings, you must have been enrolled in the pension plan for at least five years. The tax is paid on the basis of ten years. It is calculated as if you were single, with no exemptions or standard deductions and received taxable income equal to 10 percent of the lump-sum payment total. The quotient is multiplied by ten.

Example (based on an actual case history so the dollars are different): In 1981, Dr. L. received $100,000 from his pension plan. His tax base is $2,300 plus 10 percent of $100,000: $12,300. From Schedule X of Form 1040, he finds that the tax is $1,915: $1,555 plus 24 percent of the amount over $10,800. He multiplies $1,915 by 10 to get $19,150—his full tax payment. Now he has $80,850 to invest.

This calculation ignores any savings made before 1974. When distributed, these will be taxed as a long-term capital gain so the total tax will be lower. With the new tax rate, the specific tax is shown for 1982 and will be lower in the future (see table 7–1). This method is not available for IRA payouts.

Table 7–1.   Tax Rates on Ten-year Averaging: 1982

Lump-Sum Payment	Effective Tax Rate*	Tax Dollars
$ 40,000	12.0%	$ 4,800
60,000	14.5	8,700
80,000	16.1	12,880
100,000	17.2	17,200
200,000	22.3	44,600
250,000	24.7	61,750

* Ignores capital gain treatment for pre-1974 portion of distribution.
N.B. With lower tax rates in the future, rates and dollars will be less.

SOURCE: Internal Revenue Service.

Death Benefit Exclusion

With pensions under Keogh or corporate plans, the first $5,000 of a lump-sum distribution is tax free to the beneficiary if the participant dies before receiving the pension.

Tax-exempt Bonds

After retirement, your taxes, when you are in a relatively high tax bracket, may not be lower than you paid while working. It may pay you to shift from taxable to tax-exempt holdings with some of your assets.

Example: Dr. M. and his wife, both over 65, retire with assured income of $50,000: $11,000 from Social Security, $19,000 from his pension plan and $20,000 from taxable bonds. After exemptions and deductions, he pays taxes at a 35 percent rate, about $13,650 a year.

The $20,000 from the bonds represents a 12 percent yield on holding of $167,000. These were bought, over the years, at a cost of $200,000. If Dr. M. sells, he will take a loss of $33,000.

But if he does sell and reinvests the proceeds in tax-exempt bonds with a 10 percent yield, he will have $3,300 less gross income but his tax rate will drop to about 19 percent. His tax will be approximately $3,600 so he will save some $10,000 and end up with more spendable income.

In a little over three years, the tax savings will offset the loss. And, if the sales are spaced out, he can use $3,000 a year to offset $1,500 of other income. If he purchases municipals at a discount, the appreciation will be about the same as that of the taxable bonds if they were held.

These are rough figures for illustration only. Before you take such a step, consult your tax adviser. *N.B. If Dr. M. had checked earlier, he probably would not have owned so many bonds!*

Tax Benefits from Sale of Home

This is probably the biggest tax break for older folks. For those over age 55, there is no tax on the first $125,000 of profits from the sale of a home occupied for three of the last five years.

Since 80 percent of retirees own their home (and most are mortgage free), this means that they can count on a large sum which can be invested or used to buy a smaller house.

State Income Taxes

Generally, the same benefits are available with state income taxes: double exemptions, no taxes when income is low; deductions for medical costs and special treatment for retirement income. In California, for example, there's a $1,000 exemption with a reduction for every dollar of adjusted gross income: 50 percent when over $15,000.

In Florida, where there's no income tax, there are other tax advantages for the elderly: an additional $5,000 exemption on property taxes for those who have owned or occupied a residence for five consecutive years and a $25,000 exemption for certain property levies.

In South Carolina, the first $10,000 of fair market value of a dwelling owned or occupied by residents over age 65 is exempt from property taxation. When you are retired, taxes are important only if you own a lot of property or have high income. Most retirees do not and will not pay onerous taxes.

Furthermore, with the lower rates under the 1981 Economic Recovery Act, you will have more money to save for retirement. For a working couple with net taxable income of $16,000 (after all deductions/exemptions), the federal income tax will be $3,020 in 1982, $2,720 in 1983 and $2,560 in 1984. With the same income, they can count on almost $500 a year more spendable dollars (see table 7–2).

Finally, taxes on long-term gains (the kind that should be the goal of all personal investing) are lower than those of income because only 40 percent of the gain, when the property is held over twelve months, is taxed. Thus, for those in the 50 percent tax bracket, the tax rate on such profits is only 20 percent; for those in the 40 percent bracket, 16 percent.

Table 7-2.   Tax Rates for Income and Long-term Capital Gains (Joint Return)

Years	1982	1983	1984	1982	1983	1984	1982	1983	1984	1982	1983	1984
Taxable income		$16,001			$20,201			$24,601			$45,801	
Tax rate income	19%	17%	16%	25%	23%	22%	29%	26%	25%	44%	40%	38%
Long-term capital gain	7.6	6.8	6.4	10	9.2	8.8	11.6	10.4	10	17.6	16	15.2

Source: Internal Revenue Service.

8. Investing for Greatest Returns: Stocks and Annuities

Once you have set your goals, you must decide how much you can afford to invest regularly, determine the risks you are willing to take, the work you are willing to do, and the responsibilities you are willing to accept. Then, and only then, you are ready to select the investments that can be expected to build your assets while working and to assure ample income in retirement.

To a certain degree, you must choose whether you want to eat well or sleep well. With almost all investments, the options are:

- Between income and total returns (income plus appreciation). When you opt for income, you get regular, steady returns but seldom anything more.
- Between security and growth. *Security* comes from fixed asset holdings such as shares of money market funds where you can almost always get your money back or bonds which will pay off at par even though there may be interim fluctuations. *Growth* comes from quality common stocks where there can be modest income and substantial appreciation over the long term, but there will be temporary declines in market values.
- Whether you do it yourself or turn management over to someone else who will charge a fee, open or hidden, for such service.

For convenience, the following illustrations emphasize securities, but the same choices apply to other types of investments, such as real estate. Here, there are additional benefits through tax deductions for interest, taxes and depreciation. These are valuable for personal savings but seldom for tax-advantaged fiduciary funds of a pension plan.

Before retirement, set your target as a percentage return on investment: i.e., 12 percent, income (interest or dividends) from fixed income holdings; or 15 percent total returns, income plus capital gains.

After retirement, set the goal in specific dollars: i.e., if you need

$12,000 a year and have a nest egg of $100,000, the rate of return must be 12 percent.

Under no circumstances should you ever speculate with your retirement savings. Leave such risks for your personal funds.

Now let's discuss types of investments. At all times—before and after retirement—you should strive to make your money work as hard as you worked to get it in the first place (unless you are lucky enough to have received a sizeable inheritance).

The best vehicle, of course, is a pension plan with its tax deductions and tax-free accumulation. Table 8–1 shows the startling difference this shelter can make. This projection was prepared for a physician in the 50 percent tax bracket who was reluctant to set up a Keogh Plan. At that time, the maximum annual contribution was $7,500 and the anticipated yield was 10 percent. Over twenty-five years, the savings in the pension plan could be projected to grow to $737,595, as compared to $426,555, if the same sums had been made in a personal portfolio after payment of taxes. When the yields rose to 12 percent, the ultimate assets, over the same time span, could be expected to be almost double.

Table 8–1.   The Difference a Pension Plan Makes with Investment Returns

Physician, in 50% tax bracket, saves $7,500 a year. The columns show total assets at varying rates of return over different time spans: NO without a pension plan; YES with the tax advantages of a pension plan. Not shown are the benefits of lower annual income taxes due to the deductions of the contributions.

Rate of Return	Number of Years							
	10		15		20		25	
	NO	YES	NO	YES	NO	YES	NO	YES
8%	$ 94,335	$108,645	$161,850	$203,640	$247,995	$343,215	$357,960	$ 448,295
10	100,020	119,535	177,930	238,290	283,425	429,555	426,270	737,595
12	106,095	131,580	195,885	279,600	324,780	540,390	509,835	1,000,005

The calculations assume that half of the earnings in the personal portfolio were taxed as ordinary income and half as capital gains. Your own projects will be different, but regardless of your income or the rate of return, the pension plan will always be more rewarding.

Investment Approaches

Broadly speaking, there are two approaches to making money with savings: investing and speculating. With his capital:

• The investor seeks preservation first, then enhancement through income and growth in value. He looks for quality and value and recognizes the long-term benefits of compounding.

• The speculator seeks profits by taking risks, using borrowed funds and being willing to buy and sell quickly and frequently.

Most people will probably choose an in-between approach.

All savings for retirement should be invested. They are fiduciary funds, whether entrusted to someone else or managed personally. All too often, people with a little knowledge and one or two quick-profit holdings use their pension funds for trading because of the tax advantages. This can be dangerous and costly. Unless you spend a lot of time in research and review, the net profits will be small and there will be no tax benefits from losses as there are with personal portfolios.

One possible exception: a Keogh Plan whose only participants are a worker and spouse and whose assets are over $100,000. Even then, they better buy a rabbit's foot.

With personal funds, there's nothing wrong with speculating as long as you recognize the risks and use money you can afford to lose. Young people can gamble because they have time to recoup losses. But at age 55, speculators will have only ten years to catch up, let alone get ahead.

Key Investment Criteria

In successful investing, there are three key criteria: *quality, value,* and *flexibility.*

• *Quality* is like character in an individual. If one has it, one will make a mark in the community and, in his/her own way, be successful. A quality investment is secure and profitable.

• *Value* reflects the price other people are willing to pay on the basis of what they feel the future worth of the property will be. Ideally, an investment should be bought when it is undervalued and sold when it becomes fully priced.

• *Flexibility* is a general term to describe the diversification of a portfolio and the willingness of the investor to shift holdings according to changing economic conditions and future prospects.

These standards apply to all types of business enterprises, securities, real estate, and collectibles. The guidelines should be definitive and related to specific investment objectives.

To give you an idea of what to look for, here are the quality standards (digested) used by Wright Investors' Service, an international money management firm. These are minimums for corporations whose stocks are selected for the Wright Approved Investment List. They apply primarily to large companies whose shares are traded on the New York Stock Exchange, but they give you an idea of how to judge worthwhile investments. Broadly, the corporation must be financially strong with modest debt, sufficient cash and liquid assets to meet obligations, with enough shares of common stock to assure an active market and with a long, and fairly consistent, record of profitable growth: all standards required by major investors who dominate the stock market. *You can never make a profit until someone else is willing to pay a higher-than-your-cost price.*

Investment Acceptance
- Market value of publicly held shares: $50 million
- Annual trading volume: $25 million
- Annual turnover of shares: less than 50 percent
- Ownership by at least 15 institutions
- Shareholders: 5,000

Financial Strength
- Total capital and surplus: $50 million
- Equity capital (common stock) as percentage of total capital: 50 percent
- Long-term debt as percentage of total capital: 40 percent maximum
- Working capital (ratio of current assets to current liabilities): 2:1
- Convertible securities: maximum of 30 percent of outstanding common stock

Profitability
- Profit rate (PR), return on equity capital: 11 percent
- Dividends as percentage of earnings: 10 percent minimum; 75 percent maximum

Growth
- Earned growth rate (EGR): + 4 percent
- Growth in earnings: + 4 percent
- Growth in dividends: + 4 percent
- Growth in sales/revenues: + 4 percent

Now let me explain the two most important checkpoints for long-term investments: profit rate (PR) and earned growth rate (EGR). These show the ability of corporate management to make money with the money entrusted to them by stockholders.

In calculating, the base is the book value per share of common stock. This is also called stockholders' equity. It can be found in all annual reports and in many financial analyses. Book value shows the assets behind each share of common stock: what's left over when all liabilities (accounts and taxes payable, bonds, preferred stock) are subtracted from total assets (plants, equipment, cash, investments, accounts receivable). It has little relation to the price of the stock. A manufacturer of heavy machinery will have a high per share book value; a service company, with minimal equipment, will have a low one.

To find the PR, divide the profit per share by the per share book value at the beginning of the year. Thus, if the earnings are $1.50 and the book value is $10.00, the PR is 15 percent.

The same formula is used with the EGR. Start with the per share profit, subtract the per share dividends, then divide by the per share book value: i.e., $1.50 per share profit minus 50 cents per share dividends leaves $1.00 per share. Divide this by the $10 per share book value to get the EGR of 10 percent.

A top-quality company should have an annual average PR of 15 percent and EGR of 10 percent (but lower rates are acceptable with established firms and regulated corporations such as utilities).

These figures are important because they can be used to make projections of future value. When that net $1 per share is reinvested for new plants, equipment, research, products and markets, it grows tax free. In seven years, with that 10 percent reinvestment, everything will double: on a per share basis, the book value will be $20; earnings, $3; and dividends to at least $1. Such performance will boost the value of the stock, hopefully soon in anticipation; certainly, later. Roughly, the average annual rate of total return on such an investment will be over 20 percent.

For information on these checkpoints, ask your broker or consult reports of statistical services. Only about 20 percent of all New York Stock Exchange stocks meet these standards.

Table 8–2 lists some of the most profitable, fastest-growing corporations. Note how those dividends keep rising. These are the types of investments for every pension plan.

One easy way to check quality is to use the ratings set by Standard & Poor's stock guide: A+, highest; A, high; A−, above average; B+, average. Any company rated below B+ is a speculation.

Warning: Always keep checking the quality, profitability, and growth of the company whose shares you own or plan to buy. Even the best of corporations run into problems, and, temporarily, lose their investment attraction.

Value

Strong performance raises the worth of the company, but such progress is not always reflected in the market price of its stock. Once Wall Street sours on an industry or a company, it can be years before its stocks become popular again. You have to be patient. That's easy with pension plans but difficult with personal holdings.

The best time to buy any security is when it is undervalued and corporate prospects are bright and the stock is attracting investor attention as shown by higher volume and a rising price. The best time to sell a security is when it becomes overvalued.

There's no certain way to determine these points, but there are handy ways to project future values and to set target prices. These should be used only as frames of reference and should be modified according to market conditions.

Future Value

One logical way to make projections of what a stock may be worth in the future is to use two readily available figures:

1. *Price/earnings ratio (P/E).* This is the price of the stock divided by the per share earnings for the most recent twelve months. This shows how much investors are willing to pay for each dollar of profits. Thus, if the stock is selling at 24 and the just-reported annual earnings were $3 per share, the P/E ratio is 8. In late 1981, that was about the average for stocks listed on the New York Stock Exchange. In past years, this multiple has been as high as 20 and as low as 6.

P/Es vary according to the type of industry. Over the 1971–80 decade, for stable utilities it was 8.7–7.1; for fast-growing, profitable drug and electronics firms, 24–12; and heavy machinery manufacturers, 14–7.

When an industry group (and occasionally an individual company), becomes popular, its P/E will rise.

2. *Earnings growth.* If a corporation keeps boosting its profits by 10 percent a year, the price of its stock should keep pace, not always

Table 8–2.   Quality Companies with Records of Strong Growth and Profitability: Ten Years

Company	Earned Growth Rate	Profit Rate	Earnings Growth	Dividend Increase
Alco Standard	16.0%	21.4%	+13%	.15 to .74
AMP, Inc.	18.7	25.2	+18	.21 to 1.00
Archer-Daniels-Midland	15.6	17.4	+19	.08 to .12
Automatic Data Processing	17.3	21.6	+22	Nil to .37
Avnet, Inc.	15.5	19.7	+22	.20 to .86
Baker International	19.2	23.1	+27	.09 to .38
Bandag, Inc.	18.9	22.8	+22	Nil to .70
Belco Petroleum	18.2	21.4	+19	.08 to .53
Blue Bell, Inc.	15.7	21.1	+18	.31 to 1.80
Consolidated Freightways	15.1	20.8	+16	.50 to 1.38
Cooper Industries	16.9	22.8	+20	.35 to 1.08
Crown Cork & Seal	16.3	16.3	+15	Nil
Deluxe Check Print	16.9	27.1	+17	.17 to .75
Digital Equipment	16.8	16.8	+29	Nil
Dover Corporation	18.2	24.1	+20	.09 to .48
Dresser Corporation	16.1	20.7	+16	.35 to .58
Edison Brothers	15.6	22.2	+18	.33 to 1.32
E.G. & G., Inc.	17.4	21.6	+33	.05 to .43
Fort Howard Paper	18.6	25.1	+22	.13 to .78
Grainger (W.W.)	15.8	20.6	+18	.25 to .98
Halliburton Co.	17.7	22.5	+25	.17 to 1.05
Helmerich & Payne	18.4	20.3	+27	.02 to .19
Hewlett-Packard	16.8	18.7	+26	.05 to .20
Houston Natural Gas	19.7	26.1	+26	.17 to 1.30
Loctite Corp.	24.8	29.4	+21	.05 to .56
Longs Drug Stores	17.1	22.6	+15	.19 to .82
Louisiana Land	16.8	29.5	+12	.09 to 1.80
Lubrizol Corp.	17.1	26.4	+18	.21 to .90

Company			
Masco Corporation	18.0	+23	.09 to .72
MCA Incorporated	16.1	+24	.23 to 1.50
Medtronic, Inc.	19.1	+30	Nil to .52
Melville Corp.	18.2	+18	.40 to 1.60
National Medical Care	19.9	+64	Nil to .43
NCH Corporation	17.2	+18	.15 to .72
Nucor Corporation	20.4	+42	Nil to .42
Petrolane, Inc.	19.4	+19	.08 to .35
Pioneer Corp.	19.9	+28	.17 to .75
Raytheon Corp.	15.4	+19	.15 to 1.05
Revco D.S.	15.8	+19	.09 to .60
Rite Aid Corp.	16.1	+24	.06 to .54
Rollins, Inc.	18.0	+14	.07 to .42
Schering-Plough	16.6	+17	.47 to 1.56
Schlumberger, Ltd.	25.3	+34	.06 to .63
Smith International	18.3	+31	.10 to .62
SmithKline Corp.	18.8	+20	.50 to 1.73
Snap-On Tools	15.4	+17	.18 to .83
Standard Brands Paints	15.2	+15	.20 to .70
Sundstrand Corp.	16.2	+25	.40 to 1.50
Super Valu Stores	18.4	+22	.12 to .38
Tektronix, Inc.	15.0	+19	.05 to .88
Texas Oil & Gas	27.3	+33	Nil to .16
Warner Communications	17.4	+17	.07 to .51
Waste Management	18.0	+35	Nil to .28

SOURCE: Wright Investors' Service, Bridgeport, Conn.

immediately but, usually over a period of time.

To project future value, start with the current stock price and P/E ratio; find the average annual rate of growth in earnings; and use your calculator . . . as shown in table 8–3.

Table 8–3.   Future Value of a Quality Stock
(stock at 24; projected earnings growth per year: +10%)

Year	Earnings Per Share	Projected Price at P/E Ratio of:				
		8	9	10	11	12
1	$3.00	24	27	30	33	36
2	3.30	26½	29¾	33	36¼	39⅝
3	3.63	29	32⅝	36	40	43½
4	3.99	32	36	40	43⅞	47⅞
5	4.39	35⅛	39½	44	48¼	52⅝

The stock is at 24; its per share profits are $3 and its rate of earnings growth, for the past decade, has ranged between 15 percent and 8 percent. To be conservative, let's assume a future average annual rise in earnings of 10 percent. Thus, the year 2 profits could be $3.30; year 3, $3.63, etc. Generally, it's wise to project no more than five years.

With the same P/E of 8, the market price of the stock should go up to 26½ in year 2, to 29 in year 3, etc. If there's a strong market, the multiple can go higher so the price will be better: with a P/E ratio of 9, from 29¾ to 39½.

As a goal, shoot for a gain of 50 percent. With this stock, bought at 24, the target price should be 36. At that time, you can review the situation and decide whether the future rewards outweigh the risks. When any stock moves much above its established pattern, watch out. Unless there's a strong market, there may be a dip.

Be realistic. If the overall market falters or flops, your stock is not likely to rise. But as long as the corporation maintains high, profitable growth, its stock will become more valuable . . . eventually.

What if the stock price falls because of lower earnings or a bear market? Unless you are many years from retirement, sell and reinvest the proceeds in a more rewarding security. In investing, it is just as important not to lose money as to make a profit. The first loss is almost always the least expensive. This can be a tough decision, but it's wise most of the time. If you are convinced that the decline is temporary and unjustified, hang on, but my experience is that it's a good idea to sell at about 15 percent below your cost or the recent high: at about 20 for the stock bought at 24; at about 31 if the price jumps to 36.

One way to force action is to let the market make the decision by giving your broker a stop-loss order at a fraction of a point above your bail-out price: 20¼ or 31⅛, for the examples above. Most people sell or buy at a round figure so the order may be executed before the rush.

To protect profits, raise the stop-loss figure as the stock moves up: at 34¼ when it reaches 38, etc.

Common Stocks for Best Total Returns

Over the many years of a pension plan, quality stocks will provide the best returns. They GROW: in income and value. With proper selection and intelligent management, there will be no risk. If a major quality corporation has been paying dividends for fifty years and continues to make money, what's there to worry about?

True, the prices of common stocks will fluctuate—on the average, 25 percent a year between high and low price, but as long as the company prospers, the stock will be worth more . . . eventually. With the poor stock markets of recent years, it's easy to forget that over the last thirty years, from 1952 to 1981, the Dow Jones Industrial Average has risen from 270 to 1020 and after several declines has been bouncing around the 860 mark. More recently, 1970–79, the total cumulative returns on common stocks were +65.8 percent while those of corporate bonds were +7.5 percent and Treasury bills were +6.3 percent.

When you pick a winner, the gains can be substantial. The smart investor who bought 100 shares of Schlumberger, Ltd., in 1969, enjoyed five stock splits and watched his holdings grow to 1,600 shares. Their dollar value, per share (adjusted) rose from 3½ to 131—from $350 to $209,600; and dividends were up from 9 cents to 97 cents per share.

Over the same period, Caterpillar Tractor, not exactly a swinger, bought at 20 (adjusted for a split) soared to 64 and per share dividends went up from 80 cents to $2.40.

Other Types of Investments

There are, of course, many other types of worthwhile investments. Most of them provide income rather than growth, but at times, you can count on both. Before you make any commitment, check with your banker/broker/tax adviser for full details because, these days, changes can come fast and frequently.

The following examples concentrate on holdings that provide income from interest and/or dividends and, on occasion, appreciation.

This criterion eliminates almost all investments that benefit from depreciation, tax credits, payments for taxes and interest, etc.: oil wells, equipment leases, and many types of real estate. These may have merit for personal savings but seldom for tax-advantaged pension plans.

Fixed Income: where the income, usually interest, is paid regularly and the principal/face value is paid in full at some future date. In most cases, these are loans so they should be selected on the basis of the quality of the issuer.

The safest debt issues are those of the U. S. government: Treasury bills, notes, and bonds; agency bonds or mortgages insured or guaranteed by Uncle Sam; and savings accounts/certificates in bank and thrift institutions.

Next come well-rated corporate bonds. These are classified, by statistical services, from AAA(Aaa) for gilt-edged; AA(Aa), high quality; A(a), upper medium grade; BBB(Baa), medium grade; down to C, highly speculative. *Never invest in any debt rated below A!*

For convenience, let's divide the major types of debt issues by maturities: the stated life span of the security.

Short-term: due in one year or less.

Treasury bills (T-bills). These mature in ninety-one days, six months and one year. The minimum face value is $10,000, but smaller units can be traded in the after-market.

T-bills are sold on a discount basis: i.e., a one-year bill with a 15 percent yield costs $8,500. You get $10,000 at maturity. Since the 15 percent return is based on $8,500, the real yield is 17.64 percent. There will be no tax when the bills are held in a pension plan but with personal savings, this gain is considered taxable interest.

Certificates of deposit (CDs). These are available from financial institutions with yields pegged to that of the latest 6-month T-bill. Those that mature in 180 days require a minimum purchase of $10,000; those for 30 months can be bought with as little as $100.

With both, interest is compounded daily so your returns will be higher (as your friendly banker will emphasize in signs, ads and folders).

Get all the facts and be cautious:

1. There are penalties for early withdrawal, usually, the loss of all interest and a return to the low savings account interest rate.

2. Make certain that, at maturity, the new investments have your O.K. It's easy, and profitable, for the institution to roll your money over into a lower-yielding CD or, in some cases, back to a savings account.

3. Stay flexible and get locked into long-term commitments ONLY when you are convinced that the current yields are substantially higher than those anticipated in the future. A few years ago, the big "bargain" for Keogh Plans sponsored by thrift institutions was the eight-year, 8 percent account. When yields soared to over 15 percent, what once appeared to be a munificent return proved to be a disaster!

Money Market Funds. These are investment companies that sell shares and invest your money in short-term liquid assets such as Treasury bills and notes, CDs, commercial paper, bankers' acceptances, repurchase agreements, and so forth.

They pay interest daily, so you benefit from compounding. Their yields follow interest rates by three to six months. As holdings mature, they invest the proceeds in new securities: at higher returns when the cost of money rises; at lower yields when it declines.

Money market funds can be rewarding investments when yields are high but, basically, they should be regarded as parking places while you wait for long-term opportunities.

At this writing, there have been no problems with the stability of money market funds, but if just one major corporation—here or abroad —defaults on its loans, there can be serious trouble . . . fast.

Stick with quality as indicated by the reputation of the sponsor and the composition of the portfolio. For maximum safety, buy shares of funds that invest only in U. S. government securities!

And watch those yields. When they drop below 12 percent, start switching to bonds to lock in high returns and/or to common stocks if the market is moving up.

Medium-term (1–10 years); **long-term** (11–30 years). Here again, the safest investments are U. S. government issues. They are widely traded, pay semiannual interest at competitive rates and will be redeemed at face value.

You'll have a wider choice with corporate bonds rated A or better.

With direct purchases, it's difficult to take advantage of compounding because the interest checks are seldom large enough to warrant new purchases. To handle this situation:

(1) channel all interest into shares of a money market fund until there's enough capital with the addition of new savings to make a sizeable purchase—usually a slow, tedious process; or (2) buy shares of a bond mutual fund and arrange for automatic reinvestment of all

income. You'll get the compounding but may have to pay a commission of from 4.5 percent to 8.5 percent, so not all your money will go to work.

Bonds. In buying bonds, work backward: first, select the maturity date when you plan to withdraw money, usually at retirement; then, find the highest yield; and, finally, look at the price.

Now you have these choices:

New Issues. With these, you pay the full $1,000 or $5,000 per bond (slightly lower under some conditions). Since the prices of bonds move opposite to the cost of money, the market value will (1) drop when interest rates rise; (2) go up when interest rates go down. You will always get your semiannual interest but the worth of your investment will fluctuate.

Examples: In 1973, a neighbor bought 8 percent utility bonds for $10,000. By 1981, when interest rates were over 15 percent, those bonds were trading at 55 ($550) so the value of these savings was cut almost in half.

In 1981, he bought a new issue of Commonwealth Edison at par, 16¾ percent, 2011. He locked in a good yield for 30 years, and if interest rates should drop below 12 percent, each bond will be trading at about 150 ($1,500).

But if interest rates rise, he'll have another paper loss.

Discount Bonds. These are older issues that are selling well below par because of higher interest rates: New York Telephone 8 percent, 2008 at 53 ($530). The current yield is 15 percent and, in twenty-nine years, there will be sure appreciation of $470 per bond—somewhat less if cashed in earlier.

With all bonds:

• Try to buy in units of ten or more from your broker's inventory. This will save $20 to $30 per bond.

• Be slow to swap bonds, to sell losers and buy those with higher yields and shorter maturities. The losses are deductible with personal portfolios but not with pension plans.

• Make certain you understand the risks and rewards. In the twenty years between 1961 and 1980, the yields to maturity of quality bonds rose from 4.3 percent to 14 percent. The long-term bond, sold at $1,000, dropped below $400. You will always get interest payments, but they may no longer be competitive and, with inflation, will be worth less over the years.

• Buy only quality bonds when the yields are high—generally, over

14 percent. Capital gains, with their lower tax rate, may be valuable for personal savings but not for pension portfolios.

Only in periods of high yields are bonds (or any other debt issue) worthwhile investments. Their income and principal will always be diminished by inflation. But some folks prefer security and sleep better with bonds even though their assets may be waning and their income buying less.

Special Bonds for Retirement and Savings

These are U. S. government debt securities. Their yields are small and their terms restrictive. They are poor investments, but there may be improvements in the future. There are two groups:

Government Retirement Bonds. These are issued in denominations of $50, $100 and $500 through Federal Reserve Banks and the U. S. Treasury. They are designed for investments of funds in IRAs. They pay 9 percent compounded semiannually. The best that can be said for them is that they are safe.

Savings Bonds: EE and HH. EE bonds are sold at 50 percent of face value: i.e., a $50 one costs $25. They pay 9 percent when held for eight years. They cannot be cashed in until after the first six months and the maximum annual purchase, by an individual or pension fund, is $15,000 face value. When swapped for HH bonds, the interest can be deferred until the bonds are cashed in.

HH bonds are sold in denominations of $500 to $10,000, mature in ten years and pay 8.5 percent semiannually. There's a penalty for early redemption when bought for cash but not when exchanged for EE bonds. Maximum annual investment is $20,000. You must report interest annually but do not have to pay taxes until you cash in—with personal savings only.

This is one time when it does not pay to be patriotic.

Options, Calls

There are many other types of securities, but only a few are suitable for fiduciary investments and then only under special conditions. However, there is one area that can be useful for those who have ample savings —before or after retirement—and are willing to learn the techniques, do their homework and set income above appreciation. These are options, specifically calls: the right to buy a specified number of shares (usually 100) of a specified stock at a specified (striking) price before a specified expiration date.

In most cases, options are too speculative to be used in retirement plans or after-work investments, but experienced investors can use them to boost income and force profitable sales. Since all profits on all options are short-term, taxes must be considered. In a pension plan, of course, there are no taxes to be paid on these transactions. That's why writing calls for extra income can be worthwhile, and after retirement when taxes are low, may be a wise technique.

Example: In his pension plan, Dr. T. has 400 shares of Foxy Electro-Computer (FEC). They were bought at 12 and, in October, are trading at 24. FEC pays a tiny 20 cents per share dividend so Dr. T. wants more income. He is willing to sell the shares at 25 but is fearful that the market may drop soon. He writes (sells) 4 May calls at a striking price of 25 for 3 ($300 each). He receives $1,200 cash. Here's what could happen: If the stock price stays below 25 by the May exercise date, the calls will not be exercised. Dr. T. keeps the $1,200 (minus commissions) plus two dividends and in June writes new calls. If FEC stock jumps to 28 before mid-May, the calls will be exercised. Dr. T. must deliver the shares at 25. With the premium, he gets the equivalent of $28 per share. But if the stock goes higher, he won't get the extra gain.

Writing calls can be most useful after retirement because it can provide added income. By writing calls the first of every month, the investor can boost his income by as much as 15 percent . . . if he is smart, consistent and lucky.

But (1) you accept a sure, modest return rather than a potentially greater profit if the stock price rises; (2) you can lose money if the price of the stock drops sharply: with FEC, below 21, the base price of 24 minus the 3 per share premium.

Forcing a Sale. Most people are reluctant to sell securities when they have a profit. They keep hoping there will be a further gain. Calls can make that decision for you. You write a call at, or slightly below, the current price of the stock. If the call is exercised, you must sell (unless you are so optimistic that you buy back the call, probably at a price higher than you received).

Example: Bill S. bought XYZ at 19. By October, it's up to 34½. Bill is nervous so he writes a January call at 30 for 7 ($700). If the price of the stock stays well above 30, he will be forced to sell and will get the equivalent of 37—the 30 selling price plus the 7 premium. The buyer of the call makes the decision for Bill.

Before you let your broker talk you into options, get all the facts, calculate the real return (premium minus commissions and plus dividends paid while you still own the stock), and test out your ideas on paper for several months. Even with tax benefits of a pension plan, you will usually do better with straight investments. But you won't have as much fun!

Tax-exempt Bonds—for Personal Savings Only

These are debt issues of states, local governments and certain public authorities. Their interest is exempt from federal income taxes and from state and local income levies when the bonds are issued in that state. *Exception:* Puerto Rico bonds are fully exempt in all fifty states.

These are never suitable for pension plans because they duplicate the tax-free benefits, but when you have personal savings that may not be needed before retirement or are already contributing the maximum to pension plans, these municipal securities can be worthwhile.

The value of tax exempts depends on your income tax bracket. Roughly, they are profitable when you pay at a rate of 37 percent or higher. Then, a 10 percent tax-free yield is equivalent to 15.87 percent taxable return, to 16.39 percent in New York City where there are local and state income levies.

Again, stick to bonds rated A or better; buy new issues only when their yields are high; look for discount bonds with convenient maturities; and deal with a reputable broker who makes a market in the issues you purchase.

N.B. The attraction of tax exempts will dwindle in the years ahead because of lower tax rates. The 50 percent tax rate, for a couple filing jointly, applies to income of $85,600 in 1982, to $109,400 in 1983 and to $162,400 in 1984, and thereafter.

Investment Companies

If you prefer to let someone else handle your investments, you have to pay for the privilege (except with savings-related accounts), but usually, there will be offsetting advantages: diversification, convenience, special services and, increasingly, superior performance.

With employer-funded pension plans, you have no choice. With thrift institutions, you can select the type of investment at the outset but can make no changes without penalties until they mature. With insurance company annuities, you have limited choices, primarily between fixed and variable income. With investment companies, you have a wide variety of selections and, in most cases, can switch when your objectives, or economic conditions, change.

For convenience, let's concentrate on investment companies. Their operations are similar to those of life insurance companies and, in a broad sense, to those of corporate/government pension plans and common trust funds. But there can be significant differences, so be sure to get full information before you turn over your savings to anyone else.

Investment companies (often called mutual funds although this definition applies only to open-end funds) sell shares and pool the receipts for investments keyed to specific goals. For this, they charge fees, sometimes clearly stated but, more likely, included in operational costs. All shares are liquid either by redemption on demand or by sales through regular stock trading channels.

Investment companies can be divided into two types in two ways: by structure and by sales acquisition costs.

Open-end funds (mutual funds) stand ready to sell new shares or to redeem old ones at net asset value (the current worth of the underlying securities).

Closed-end funds are similar to corporations. They have a fixed number of shares, often listed on major stock exchanges, that are bought and sold like regular stocks with standard commissions. Their values fluctuate according to investor attitudes. In recent years, they have been selling at discounts of 10 percent to 25 percent from net asset values.

All funds can also be categorized as:

Load funds. These are sold, primarily by registered representatives of brokerage firms but also by qualified-by-law individuals who work full- or part-time.

The sales charge, typically about 8.5 percent (lower with larger purchases), is deducted from the amount of the investment so you have less money working for you. But the sales representative handles all details.

No-load funds. These are bought directly from the sponsor with no sales charge.

With both load and no-load funds, there is no cost for redeeming the shares. Management fees run from 0.5 percent of the value of the invested money.

Principal Types of Investment Companies

Investment companies come in all sizes, shapes and combinations. You can find one for almost every objective and type of security/property. For retirement savings, these are the ones to be considered:

Stock funds:

• For income: investments in preferred stocks, common stocks that pay high dividends and, at times, bonds and convertibles.
• For balance: holdings in a mix of fixed income securities and of quality common stocks.
• For growth: investments with the potential of long-term appreciation in a mix of shares of major companies and smaller corporations "with a future."

Convertible funds: portfolios of convertible bonds and preferred stocks with some stocks acquired through conversion.

Bond funds: fixed income securities, primarily government and corporate bonds. There are two types:

• *Unit trusts:* closed-end funds that invest the entire proceeds of an offering in bonds and make no changes. As the bonds are called or mature, distributions are made. These funds are self-liquidating so that when assets drop to about 20 percent of the original investment, the fund goes out of business.
• *Managed funds:* open-end funds that buy and sell bonds according to projections of the trend of interest rates. If the managers guess right, they can be quite profitable; if they guess wrong, you can lose a bundle.

These two types of bond funds are available for both taxable and tax-exempt securities.

Money market funds are described under fixed income investments on p. 91.

There are a score of other types of funds: *performance* for trading; *special situations* for high-risk holdings; *high-yielding bond funds* that invest in marginal debt securities; *commodities funds* that trade futures contracts; *option funds* that buy and sell calls and puts, and so forth. Few of these are suitable for retirement savings.

Advantages of Investment Companies

1. *Diversification.* Unless you have $50,000, it is almost impossible to have a properly diversified portfolio. With all funds, you own a portion of shares in twenty or thirty companies. This lessens the losses but also inhibits the gains which, usually, come from a few big winners.

2. *Systematic supervision.* Management companies have the personnel, research, facilities and experience to handle all details of security transactions, interest and dividend payments, rights, proxy statements, etc. Income can be reinvested promptly for compounding or distributed periodically. You also get accurate year-end summaries for income tax purposes.

3. *Professional management.* While the performance of some funds leaves something to be desired, the majority of investment companies have done as well, or slightly better, than the overall market. The money managers are professionals who have strict standards of selection and, generally, make their decisions on facts rather than emotions.

4. *Switching privileges.* You have the right to move from one type of fund to another under the same management: from growth to income when yields are rising; vice versa when they fall.

5. *Beneficiary designation.* You can name a beneficiary under a trust agreement so that the fund assets will avoid probate at the death of the owner.

6. *Open account.* This provides the right to invest whenever you have extra savings. The money buys shares immediately and avoids the bother of separate certificates for small or fractional shares.

7. *Regular income checks.* These can be paid by month, quarter or other specified period. This can be handy for retirement. If you arrange for payment of a fixed sum, you will get it because the fund will sell some shares.

8. *Loan program.* The shares are available as collateral for loans at interest rates tied to the broker's call money rate. Typically, the minimum loan is $5,000 on a 50 percent margin. There are no set repayment terms, and you can defer interest by raising your debt balance.

Almost all investment companies will set up retirement plans and handle all details of investing and data needed for reporting.

Guidelines for Choosing Funds

Funds should be selected for a specific objective of income or growth. Here are checkpoints:

Performance. This is the key. You want to know how effectively the fund has achieved its stated goal. The record should cover at least five and, preferably, ten years so that it included both up and down markets.

An income fund should have produced yields comparable to those available from T-bills. A growth fund should have total average annual returns—income plus appreciation—that have been 2 percent more than that of a quality bond—15 percent when fixed income holdings yield 13 percent.

Pay attention to that average. A fund may be a big winner one year but a poor performer the next. Look for the fund's record in both bull and bear markets. In up years, the fund should beat the market; in down years, the losses, if any, should not be greater than that of a major average: for stocks, the Dow Jones Industrials or Standard & Poor's 500 Stock Average; for bonds, the Dow Jones Bond Average.

Investment portfolio. What types of stocks does the fund hold? When were they bought? When are they sold? And how wide is the diversification to assure balance?

A fund that holds a lot of cash after the start of a confirmed bull market is not making the best use of its money.

A fund whose holdings are dominated by big name favorites (Exxon, GE, IBM) is buying reputation and security. You can do as well yourself.

If the names of some of the stocks are unfamiliar, management is speculative minded. The fund may do well for a short time, but the odds of long-term success are against you.

Watch the timing in different types of markets. Did the fund sell Avon at 140 or 19? Did it buy Schlumberger, Ltd. at 5 (adjusted) or at 50?

When a fund becomes huge (over $500 million), management is restricted to investments in a few major companies whose shares are likely to be slow to rise and fast to fall. These big funds seldom beat the market average because, in a sense, they are the market.

On the other hand, beware of funds with small assets (under $50 million). If they are new, there's no track record. If they are established, why haven't they grown more rapidly?

Turnover. This shows the dollar amount of stocks sold in relation to total assets. Thus, for a fund that has assets of $100 million and sells $75 million in stocks in one year, the turnover is 75 percent. This is high and indicates that the managers are either speculating for short-term profits or trying to correct mistakes. The best funds are those that are slow to buy and sell and hold their portfolios longer than the funds as a group.

Real Estate

In broad terms, real estate investments include properties (land, commercial buildings, apartments, etc.) owned outright or as a limited partner. They are best for personal holdings because of the ample deductions against income of depreciation, interest payments, real estate taxes and investment tax credits. They are suitable for pension plans when bought for income and appreciation.

The tax benefits of a pension plan can be used for extra profits. In effect, the pension plan swaps the depreciation benefits for greater income and, at sale or refinancing, a larger share of the realized gains.

Example: The Keep 'Em Well Professional Corporation (KEWP), owned by a group of physicians, has $2 million in its pension fund. The doctors are willing to invest $400,000 in real estate if they can count on a minimum yield of 12 percent plus 100 percent appreciation in six years (an annual compounded rate of 15 percent).

Builder Bill finds a lot on which he wants to erect a store/office building. He has a substantial mortgage commitment but, like most developers, lacks cash.

Here's how KEWP can benefit: with pension plan money, KEWP buys the land and arranges with Bill and his partners for (1) payment of annual interest of not less than $60,000 or 12 percent of the rental income which can be projected to increase; (2) a set percentage of the price at which the building is refinanced or sold.

In return, KEWP turns over to the limited partnership all depreciation and tax credits. Since these investors are all in high tax brackets, they get extra tax deductions.

Real estate is too complex a subject to be explained in detail but here are some guidelines for including property in pension plan portfolios:

• When fund assets are adequate enough to permit a minimum investment of $25,000 which, in turn, is no more than 20 percent of total investments. With success and experience, this percentage can be raised.

• When income yields are competitive with those of government securities and can be expected to increase.

• When funds will not be needed for at least five years. With all real estate, it is easier to get in than to get out.

• When the investment manager understands what's happening and deals with reputable people and well-located property.

Despite what you read in books that tell you "How I Made a Million Dollars in Real Estate," it's a tough, tricky business. With all real estate, be skeptical:

- Increase the anticipated costs of building by 20 percent
- Reduce the projected income by 25 percent
- Lengthen the period of a profitable payout by 30 percent

Still, in the right area, with the right property and the right management, real estate investments can be rewarding. The most important factor is appreciation which, in turn, depends on location.

Investing Retirement Funds

With the broader IRAs, started in 1982, came a flood of investment "opportunities" from brokers, bankers, thrift institutions, insurance companies, etc. They all want your money and offer what, at first, appears to be rewarding results. Generally, however, the real returns are more convenient (and promotional) than profitable. The ads trumpet high yields but only rarely are these guaranteed for any long period of time, and nothing is said about the terms of withdrawal.

Yet the difference in rates of return can be significant over the life of a retirement plan. A 2 percent higher yield, with compounding, can be dramatic:

With a lump-sum investment of $10,000:

Single Investment—$10,000

	Total	
Annual Yield	10 Years	20 Years
10%	$25,900	$67,300
12%	31,000	96,500
Difference	+ 5,100	+29,200

With an annual investment of $1,000 (in a personal pension plan):

Annual Investment—$1,000

10%	15,940	57,270
12%	17,550	72,050
Difference	+1,610	+14,780

In deciding where to put your personal pension contributions, look at both ends: what happens when you put in your savings and when you start withdrawals after work. The longer and more fully you remain in control, the more rewarding will be the results (assuming you use common sense). When someone else takes charge, there will be costs, open or hidden, that will shave your yields and, later, income. There's no free lunch.

To give you an idea of how cosmetic the offers are, take a look at these offers for IRAs made in Florida in early 1982 (see table 8–4).

But these are come-ons and tell only half the story. You should KNOW how you will get your money back after retirement. The institution emphasized how much you may have, but only one of ten money managers could explain how withdrawals would be made and that was based on a copy of an annuity table torn from a statistical publication.

If possible, always arrange for choices on payouts. The most convenient type of withdrawal (and usually the least rewarding), is a lifetime annuity. The most flexible is a lump-sum payment, which can be reinvested to fit your needs.

With the small contributions of an IRA, it's difficult to invest in a high-yielding fixed-income security such as a T-bill at the outset. In most cases, the rewards will be greater with shares of a mutual fund or quality common stocks. The income will be reinvested for compounding, and with stocks, there will be appreciation . . . more than enough to offset the erosion of inflation.

Debt holdings—bills, bonds and CDs—can be safe and, often tempo-

Table 8–4.   Typical Terms for IRAs

Institution	Fees	Minimum	Plans/Yields
Atlantic Bank	$15 per year	$100	1% above 6-month CD, rate changing weekly, now 14.056%
Florida National	None	25	15% through June 1982; after that, 18-month fixed rate and variable rates available, tied to T-bill rates
American Savings	None	100	Variable rate changes weekly, now 13.1%; fixed rates for 18–30 months, now 14.75%
First of Delray	None	100	Variable rate, 20% through April 15, then tied to weekly T-bill rate; for $500 and up, can get 30-month fixed rate, now 14.75%
First of the Palm Beaches	None	100	30-month fixed rate, now 12%; variable rate changes weekly, 12.5%.
Sunrise Savings	None	10	Variable rate, changes each month, now at 13%; for $250 and up, can get fixed rate for 30 months to 4 years, now 14.75%

Mid-1982.

rarily rewarding but they are *dead* investments in that their returns are, basically, fixed, so always affected by inflation. You are sure of getting back your principal at some future date, but your principal will always be worth less.

Quality common stocks are *live* investments. Their values . . . and income . . . will grow so that, at retirement, you will have greater assets . . . and income. Keep these distinctions in mind when you invest any savings and always consider the probable total returns: without taxes with pension contributions (until withdrawal); and after taxes with personal savings.

Example: $10,000 lump sum. Choices:

1. A CD to mature in five years with interest compounded quarterly
2. Shares of a bond fund that compounds interest semiannually
3. Stock of a company that automatically reinvests dividends annually, increases earnings and dividends by 10 percent a year and has a P/E ratio of 10

The tax rate, for easy figuring, is 33 percent.

Investment	Total Income–5 Years	Tax	Net Value
CD @ 10%	$6,380	$2,127	$14,253
Bonds @ 10%	6,380	2,127	14,253
Stock: 5% dividends	2,819	846	1,973
10% growth	6,105	403*	5,702
	8,824	1,249	17,015

*Taxed at capital gains rate: 6.6%

   This is oversimplified because the value of the stock, with the same price/earnings ratio, would rise to provide greater assets.

With personal investments, taxes on income will be paid annually; with Keogh and Professional Corporation Plans, taxes will be paid only at withdrawal and can be less depending on the method of payout.

With all types of savings, pension plan or personal, make the projections at the outset and use your current tax rate for the payout. If the broker/institution cannot give you an anticipated rate of return, use an average of 10 percent for fixed income holdings. If your money earns more, you'll be ahead.

But do not anticipate that you will get those advertised 12 percent to 15 percent yields. Interest rates are likely to be lower in the years ahead, but quality common stocks can provide that 15 percent average annual rate of return.

Summary

Forget about systems and special approaches that are touted by self-styled "experts" in investment advisory letters and books. There is nothing complicated or difficult about successful investing. As long as you place quality first and are patient, you will always make out well. If you buy when the property is undervalued, prospects are bright and investor interest is growing, you will score gains soon.

And if you sell quickly when you make a mistake or the market turns down, you will keep your losses low.

Anyone who does his homework and uses common sense can make money and, with prompt reinvestment of income and realized gains for compounding, can make a lot of money and assure that financially secure retirement.

Surveys show that Mainstreet (the average intelligent investor) almost always outperforms Wallstreet (the so-called professional) over the years. Don't try to outguess the market. Just put your savings in safe, money-making situations that keep you and your spouse happy!

And to offset that ever-irritating inflation, invest according to the information summarized in table 8–5.

Annuities: For Those Who Hope to Live Long

The official definition of an annuity is a contract that provides monthly income, starting at retirement, for a specified period of time. These payments can be structured for personal or financial or psychological goals: for the life of one individual; for as long as either spouse lives; or for a certain number of years, usually ten or twenty. And they can be arranged so there's nothing left at death or undistributed assets are turned over to a beneficiary.

Annuities can be purchased at any age, by a lump sum or periodic payments. At retirement, they are usually based on one substantial investment. As a rule of thumb, at age 65, the annual income is about 12 percent: $120 per $1,000, or $1,200 a year per $10,000 for men; somewhat less for women because they live longer.

The payout on all annuities is based on average life expectancy and the risk-sharing concept that the loser pays for the winner, i.e., those who die early will provide the money for those who live beyond their actuarial death age.

These are the major choices:

Straight annuity: a regular payment for life. If it's for single cover-

Table 8–5.   How Some Investments Rate as Long-term Inflation Hedges

Investments	Practical Minimum	Approx. Yield (percentage)	Safety	Appreciation	Inflation Hedge
Common stocks	$ 1,000				
Quality		3– 8	High	Excellent	Excellent
Speculative		0–10	Poor	High	Fair
Preferred stocks	1,000	8–12	High	Small*	Poor*
Corporate bonds	5,000	12–15	High	Poor*	Poor*
Treasury bills	10,000	15	Highest	None**	None
Treasury notes	5,000	15	Highest	Poor*	Poor*
Treasury bonds	5,000	15	Highest	Poor*	Poor*
Tax-exempt bonds	5,000	10–12	High	Poor*	Poor*
Convertibles	5,000	8–10	Good	High	High
Savings account	100	5.5	Highest	None	Poor
Savings certificates	500	13–15	Highest	None	Poor
Mutual funds	1,000				
Growth		4– 6	Fair	High	Good
Income		12–14	Good	Small	Poor
Balanced		10–12	Good	Good	Fair
Money market		16	Good	None	Poor

* Appreciation only when bought below par and redeemed, at face value, at maturity
** Since bought at discount, appreciation represents interest

Source: Based on data in financial journals as of mid-1982.

age and the annuitant dies one day after the payout begins, there will be nothing left. But if you live to be 95, you will win handsomely.

Refund annuity: not quite as much income because, at the death of the participant, the remaining principal goes to a named beneficiary until the original commitment is paid out.

Period certain: medium income with payments guaranteed for a set number of years, typically ten or twenty.

Joint and last survivorship: assured income to two people as long as either lives.

With most plans, even though the original program has been set up with one insurance company, you can make a change just before retirement. This can be important because of the substantial changes, resulting from high interest rates that have been extant recently. Table 8–6 shows the data for an annuity set up with an annual contribution of $1,000 over thirty years. Terms for single payment and shorter-period savings are similar. Note how the yields and monthly payout differ. This shows why it is so important to shop before you make a final decision.

If you opt for security first and your maternal ancestors have lived four score and ten years, an annuity can be very worthwhile. But, for

Table 8–6.   Fixed-dollar Annuity Plans
(based on $1,000 annual investment)

Insurer	Recent Interest Rate	30-Year Accumulation at Recent Rate	Monthly Payout at Age 65
Bankers Life	12%	$249,412	$2,820*
Equitable Life	11.5	237,906	2,412*
Occidental Life	12.5	294,369	3,262
Provident Life	11.28	224,878	N.A.
Travelers Insurance	12.10	263,466	2,658*

* 10 years certain.

Source: Local agents.

most people, it is not the best use of savings for retirement. In most cases, there will be nothing left at the death of the surviving partner. When the same dollars are invested in bonds yielding 12 percent, you will get as much or more income while you and your spouse live and the principal will remain intact, or possibly, will appreciate.

Investment Choices

You can arrange for your money to be invested in either fixed or variable income funds. The fixed income portfolio will consist of bonds, certificates of deposit and Treasury bills; variable portfolios will be a mix of fixed income securities and common stocks.

Over a six-year period, Aetna Life reported that its variable portfolio outperformed the fixed income fund in all but one year. In 1980 the yields were as much as 23 percent higher. But with variable holdings, you always face the possibility of a loss year (see table 8–7).

Table 8–7.   Comparative Performance Annuity Funds

Year	Variable Fund	Income Shares
1975	+29.21%	+19.62%
1976	+23.28	+20.85
1977	− 2.61	+ 4.11
1978	+ 8.32	+ 1.21
1979	+19.96	+ .72
1980	+25.45	+ 1.97

Source: Aetna Life Insurance Company, Hartford, Conn.

Deferred Annuities

These are contracts that can be purchased in one lump sum or by periodic savings. They are personally financed supplements to pension plans. The savings are not tax deductible but the income accumulates tax free until withdrawal.

Table 8–8 shows the benefits. In the first year, because of the 5 percent commission, there's not much difference between the value of the annuity and a taxable investment. But as the tax-deferred income compounds, annuity becomes increasingly valuable.

At withdrawal, after 20 years, with the recipient in the 50 percent tax bracket, the tax on the $34,279 ($44,279 minus $10,000 investment) would be $17,140, leaving a *total* of $27,139. This is considerably more than the $21,911 available under the taxable investment.

In 1981, IRS knocked out the so-called wrap-around annuities that combined a family of mutual funds with an annuity umbrella to give tax deferral of income. Some companies are trying to get around the terms of this ban by setting up an insurance company managed money market fund. This is primarily an insurance investment product and does not provide the same yields, flexibility or payouts. Still, with the tax-deferred feature, the net returns are more rewarding than investments in taxable programs/securities. In the 40 percent tax bracket, a 15 percent taxable return nets to 9 percent—less than the 12 percent tax-free possible with some annuities.

Inflation Beaters

Insurance companies, mindful of the competition from money market funds and the impact of inflation on fixed income holdings, have come

Table 8–8.   How Annuities Outpace Taxable Investments*

Year	Deferred Annuity	Taxable Investment
1	$10,260	$10,400
5	13,958	12,166
10	20,509	14,802
15	30,135	18,009
20	44,279	21,911

* Based on an original $10,000, 8% yield, front-end load, for the annuity of 5%.

SOURCE: *Money Reporter,* October 24, 1980.

up with new types of annuities. Manufacturers Life, for example, offers a plan that provides guaranteed income with annual increases in payments. Life income is guaranteed for fifteen years even if the annuitant dies. Payments rise 6 percent annually for the first twelve years, then level out (see table 8–9).

Table 8–9.   Inflation-beating Annuity*

Year	Monthly Income
1	$147.31
2	156.15
5	185.98
10	248.88
12	279.64
13 and after	296.42

* $25,000 annuity. Annual increase of 6% through 12th year, level thereafter.

SOURCE: Manufacturers Life (Robert F. Harris, Millburn, N.J. 07041).

Tax Consequences

Table 8–10 shows how taxes are calculated for retirees—by an IRS formula based on anticipated life span. It is still possible to make withdrawals tax free, up to the amount of the original investment. This can be useful if you need extra money to furnish a new house after you quit work.

Example: Stuart M., aged 55, inherits $100,000. He buys a deferred annuity. At age 63, the investment has grown to over $200,000. Stu

Table 8–10.   Tax Consequences on Annuity Payouts

Mrs. H., aged 75, with a life expectancy of twelve years, buys a nonrefund annuity for $10,000. This pays her $100.62 per month. She can deduct $69.44 from each monthly payment as the tax-exempt return of capital.

Expected return from contract:	
144 months x $100.62	$14,489.28
Cost	10,000.00
Interest portion	$ 4,489.28
Monthly payment	$ 100.62
Interest portion: $4,489.28/144 months	31.18
Return of principal: $10,000/144 months	$ 69.44

withdraws $100,000 tax free as a return of capital.

The next year, before he starts retirement, he dies. Now his heirs will have to pay the income tax: with one payment if a lump sum is withdrawn; with periodic payments if the payout is spread over several years.

Checkpoints for All Annuities

Always shop around before buying any type of annuity and compare the costs and benefits. But remember that service, by the agent, can be important, especially for your heirs. A difference of $8 per month may not seem significant, but it's about $100 a year and if you live another twenty years, can amount to a sizeable sum.

Check these items:

• Sales charges: from 5 percent to 8 percent of the original investment; this is off-the-top so there's less money working for you

• Fees: from 1.5 percent to 2 percent per year

• Interest/income: the guaranteed rate of return is low, typically 4 percent, but the real return, in times of high yields, can be over 12 percent

• Tax status: usually, the income is exempt from state taxes

• Withdrawals: some allow you to take out up to 10 percent of your savings during the first seven years; others are less flexible

• Surrender charge: most have descending fees, from 7 percent in the first year to 6 percent in the second year, etc., with no fee after the seventh year

• Opportunity to switch investments: from an old contract with a low yield to a new one with a higher rate of return, usually, with no tax on capital gains of a variable annuity if the new policy, with the same company, is for a larger amount.

• Estate status: proper structuring can avoid an estate tax, attorney's fees and court costs after your death.

Annuities should be regarded as investments for retirement and should be judged by the same standards of safety, income and potential appreciation. They are always better for the sponsors and their salesmen than for the purchaser, but they are safe and secure. It's the old choice: peace of mind or rewards. As long as investment yields remain high, and pension plans provide tax deductions for contributions, go slow with purchases of annuities. The payouts are seldom more than 12 percent and, at the death of the surviving spouse, there will seldom be anything left. You can get the same, or better, return from fixed income securities and retain and, with wise selections enhance, your capital.

III.

PROTECTION FOR
FAMILY AND SELF

Basically, protection involves insurance: funds to replace income and pay final expenses at death; health insurance to help pay for medical costs; property and casualty coverage for your car, home and possessions. It is important to have the right amount of the right kind for the right period of time.

Life insurance is essential when there are children; valuable during middle age when you are building income and assets; and of decreasing importance when you are retired.

The need for health insurance lessens when you reach age sixty-five when Medicare becomes available. And the worth of property insurance depends on the impact of potential damage or loss. In all cases, the costs of protection should be weighed against the real risks and benefits.

Too often, older people are overinsured. From habit, they continue their life insurance; from fear, they increase their health protection. Yet, in most cases, coverage can be reduced to provide additional funds for daily living.

9. Life Insurance: The Full Story

The primary role of life insurance is to assure *current* benefits: at the death of the insured to make available money to bridge the gap between the income your heirs will have and that which they will need. That's why it is often wise to reduce or eliminate life insurance in after-work years.

The primary role of a pension plan is to assure *future* benefits: to provide funds during retirement. Life insurance is not permitted in an Individual Retirement Account, must be incidental in a Keogh Plan and is permissible with corporate plans under special circumstances that make the premiums a deductible corporate expense but are partially taxable to the recipient.

It is important to understand the differences between the two types of life insurance, *straight* and *term,* and the two types of insurance company investments, *fixed* and *variable.* There are, of course, combinations and variations. Usually, they are better for sales than for protection.

Straight Life Insurance

With straight life (also called whole or ordinary life), the death benefit, usually the face value of the policy, and the premium remain fixed over the years until the policy is paid up. It is possible to use the dividends, if any, to increase protection or to reduce premiums. The important point is that, each year, the cash value, reflecting your savings through payments of premiums, increases while the insurance dollars diminish. In other words, the longer the policy remains in effect, the less the liability of the insurance company.

Example: Clark K. takes out a $10,000 straight life policy and pays the first annual premium of, say, $130. If he dies the next day, his beneficiary will get $10,000. That's a high return on a modest investment.

But if Clark lives twenty years and lets the dividends accumulate, the cash value of the policy will rise to about $5,000. If he dies, his beneficiary will still get $10,000 but the death benefit—the amount for which the insurance company is responsible—will be only $5,000.

In other words, the longer the policy remains in effect, the less the liability of the insurance company.

Straight life insurance does provide permanent protection as long as the premiums are paid or until the policy is paid up, but, realistically, it's an expensive forced savings plan. It is best suited to people who are unwilling or unable to save regularly.

Term Life Insurance

Term life is like a fire insurance policy. It protects for a limited period of time at a low rate. At expiration, it's worthless, although it can usually be renewed at a higher annual cost. At age 65, however, if you still feel the need for family protection, buy straight life because, at this age, the premiums are about the same and you can get the benefits of the savings and ever-higher dividends.

Check table 9–1, and see for yourself. At age 45, a man can buy $100,000 of five-year, renewable-convertible term for $443. The same protection, with straight life, would cost six times as much: $2,758 a year. Never buy any life insurance until you have reviewed the alternatives. Annual savings of $2,000 a year, invested at 10 percent, will grow to $35,060 in ten years and to $126,000 in twenty years.

For a possible solution, consider special policies such as these:

Adjustable Life

This provides a choice of either term (with limited cash value) or straight life (with ever-higher cash values). You can adjust the mix

Table 9–1.   Approximate Cost of Term Life   (per $1,000 coverage)

Age	Male	Female
34	$ 1.94	$ 1.68
39	2.63	2.12
45	4.43	3.62
50	7.13	5.78
60	17.05	13.83
65	25.95	20.05

SOURCE: The Bankers Life Company, Des Moines, Iowa.

according to your protection needs and available savings. When you're young and short of money, you buy more term: when your income increases, you switch to straight life with higher premiums and much greater cash values.

If you run into unexpected expenses, you can reduce the premium for that year with a corresponding drop in the length of the current term-life protection period, say from ten to five years. If you get a bonus, you can increase the premium payment and broaden your coverage or shorten the payment period. Adjustable life is so flexible that, as the insurance companies advertise, "It's the only policy you'll ever need!"

Minimum Deposit Insurance

This is usually sold as a painless way to finance life insurance. You borrow against the cash value to pay premiums: i.e., if the premium is $270 and the dividend average $150, you borrow $120 from the accumulated cash value.

Like most loan-related plans, this is expensive and probably worthwhile only for those in high tax brackets where the deduction, for the interest, is significant.

Universal Life

This is a flexible, do-it-yourself combination of life insurance and a high interest savings account. One element is a renewable term policy; the other is a cash-value account resembling a money market fund. You can adjust either element to match a family's changing responsibilities and ability to pay premiums.

Example: At age 25, Charlie C. marries and pays a premium of $800 to buy a $100,000 policy. The next year, the premium portion drops and, thereafter, rises slowly each year. Cash value starts accumulating immediately and earns, say, 11 percent—guaranteed for one year.

Soon, Charlie has two children and buys a house. Now, the insurance protection is increased and the savings decreased. At its peak, such a policy would provide $244,452 coverage.

By increasing the premium whenever possible, Charlie builds cash value of $44,452 by the time the first child enters college. He withdraws $6,000 a year, at no cost as the money is taken from the cash value (his own money). He stops paying premiums at age 46. This $912 a year is also subtracted from the cash account. Once both children have finished college, Charlie boosts the annual premiums to $5,000 a year.

Assuming a constant 11 percent return (actually, not true as the yields will vary with the cost of money), the cash value will be $118,739 when Charlie reaches retirement age of 65. Now he can count on an annuity of about $14,000 and never touch the principal.

N.B. The 1982 tax law restricts the amount of tax-deferred savings, so ask your agent for details *first.*

Retired Lives Reserve (RLR)

This is an excellent choice when you work for a corporation that is willing to provide extra fringe benefits. Your company contributes regularly to a two-part policy: term insurance for current protection and a side fund that's held by an insurance company or trustee. At retirement, the side fund is tapped to provide term insurance for the rest of your life.

The entire cost is tax deductible to the company. The executive reports, as income, the annual cost of term insurance over $50,000.

Example: ABC Corporation buys a $100,000 policy for a 40-year-old male vice president at an annual cost of $2,633. The executive adds $2,633 to his taxable income: in the 50 percent tax bracket, a net cost of $1,317 a year.

At retirement at age 65, the executive has either $100,000 insurance for life or $23,400 cash value coverage. He can borrow all or part of that cash value and reduce the amount of protection (see table 9–2).

A variation of this adds a deferred compensation plan. The executive gets $100,000 life insurance and deferred compensation which, at age 65, will be worth $67,226 at an 8 percent annual yield.

The corporation pays an average of $2,642 annually: $1,767 for the insurance is tax deductible; $875 for the after-work compensation—not deductible. The executive reports, as taxable income an average of $679: a net cost, in the 50 percent tax bracket, of $339.50.

Inflation-fighting Policies

These are designed to raise the death benefits to offset some of the erosion of purchasing power. In most cases, they are more convenient than rewarding. Their costs are high; they carry ample commissions for the agent; their benefits lag behind the cost of living; but they do provide a sense of extra security when you plan to keep the policy for as long as you live. Here are some of the most popular types:

Table 9–2. Life Insurance as a Corporate Fringe Benefit

Type	Cost	At Retirement
	($100,000 straight life, paid up at age 65; executive now 40 years old)	
Life insurance paid up at age 65	Company pays $2,633 per year, tax deductible. Executive reports extra $2,633 a year income on tax return.	Executive has either: (1) $100,000 insurance for life; (2) $23,400 cash value; or (3) a loan against cash value that reduces the amount of life insurance.
RLR plus a deferred compensation plan	The company pays an average of $1,767 per year, tax deductible, plus $875 a year into deferred-compensation plan with no tax deduction. The executive reports an average of $679 a year of this as income.	The executive has $100,000 insurance for life. His deferred compensation, taxable when received, is worth a minimum of $36,813 and as much as $67,226 at 8% interest.

SOURCE: Sentry Life Insurance Company, New York, N.Y.

Automatic increases. The death benefit rises annually, typically to a limit of 15 percent, or $50,000. For a 40-year-old male, on the basis of 7 percent annual inflation, a $100,000 policy would pay off $131,079 in five years and $183,845 in ten years (see table 9–3).

Table 9–3.   Life Insurance That Keeps up with Inflation

| | ($100,000 whole life; male, age 40; annual inflation, 7%) | | |
Year	Face Amount	Annual Premium	Cash Value
1	$100,000	$1,879	$ 0
5	131,079	2,525	5,174
10	183,845	3,874	18,093
15	257,852	6,246	40,049
20	300,000	8,285	74,423
25	300,000	8,285	111,372

SOURCE: Executive Wealth Advisory, October 5, 1981.

The premiums go up, too: from an original $1,879 a year to $2,525 at the end of five years, to $3,874 in ten years. But these increases are less than the costs of separate policies purchased at the latter ages.

A variation of this is increasing whole life where the face amount rises annually to double in twenty years. Premiums are higher at the end of each five years but remain level after the twentieth year.

Adjustable life with cost-of-living agreement. By allocating more of the annual premium to the term portion, the death benefits increase every three years by 20 percent or $20,000, whichever is less.

Variable premium life. Here, the premiums fall as inflation rises. These policies are sold at a discounted price that is guaranteed for two years. Then, the premiums move up with inflation's effect on interest and expenses rates and mortality tables. You're protected to the extent that the premiums can never go above a preset ceiling.

These are a few examples of the many special policies that are now available (and new ones are coming along frequently). See your agent for details and if he does not have what you want, shop around. Before you sign up, get comparative costs and benefits. These days, the life insurance business has something for almost everyone for almost every purpose and for almost every purse. But *buy the contents, not the package.*

Finally, keep in mind that, after retirement, life insurance will become less important. At that point, most people need income more than protection.

When to Swap Policies

Keeping in mind that retirement planning with insurance should seek to keep costs low, there are situations when it pays to swap policies. This is usually because investment yields are far above the dividend rate on old policies. You will have to pay commissions on the new purchase but, with some straight life policies, a switch can be worthwhile.

Examples: Henry H., aged 49, has a straight life policy, bought some years ago, for $256,000. The annual premium is $7,244. He swaps this for a new policy, with the same death benefits, with a premium of $5,473. By age 77, he'll save over $100,000, and if the savings are invested or the dividends are compounded, he'll be able to leave twice as much for his heirs.

Charles W., aged 42, has a $50,000 straight life policy bought fifteen years ago. Its cash value is $11,000; the current premium is $858 a year and the dividend $400, so his net annual cost is $458. He surrenders the policy and uses the $11,000 to buy municipal bonds with a tax-free yield of 12 percent. Now he pockets $1,320 a year. Since he has $11,000 worth of bonds, he needs only a $40,000 policy to bring his death benefits to $51,000. This coverage costs $600 a year so he has $720 extra each year.

Keep in mind that if you swap policies, there can be extra cash—the amount saved with the lower premium—to be used as a contribution to your IRA. This will build, tax advantaged, to provide extra income after retirement. Table 9–4 shows how to make your calculations. Make the switch only if the savings are significant: as a rule of thumb, about $100 a year.

Which Policies to Drop

By the time your children are on their own, your house is probably pretty well paid for; you have accumulated other assets such as investment or vested interests in pension plans, so that your need for life insurance protection is less. This is the time to review all policies and decide which to drop. If you are reluctant to make changes, delay this decision until a couple of years before you quit work. If you wait until after retirement, any financial decisions, no matter how wise, will be difficult for most couples.

Table 9–4.   How to Determine Whether to Switch Life Insurance Policies

	Amount
1. Face value of present (old) policy	_____
2. Current cash value of old policy	_____
3. New insurance needed if old policy is cashed in (1 minus 2)	_____
4. Annual interest if cash value of old policy is invested at 12% a year	_____
5. Annual premium of old policy	_____
6. Annual premium of new policy	_____
7. Net payment on new policy (6 minus 4)	_____
8. Premium savings (5 minus 7)	_____
9. Cash value of policies at age 65:	
Old policy if continued	_____
New policy: current cash value of old policy (2) minus future cash value of new policy	_____
10. Dividends	
Old	_____
New	_____

SOURCE: C. Colburn Hardy: *Your Money & Your Life,* American Management Association, New York, N.Y., 1982.

The key calculations on which, if any, policies to drop involve the comparative returns: whether you will come out ahead by holding the present policy and its modest annual dividends (usually about 6 percent but sometimes higher) or by cashing in and investing the proceeds at a better yield: 12 percent to 15 percent a year.

The maximum death benefit from the insurance will be its face value unless you are one of those rare individuals who has used the dividends to buy additional coverage: i.e., if it's a $10,000 policy, that's what your heirs will get. If it's a straight life policy, the cash value will probably be less, say $6,000 when the insured is 60 years old.

He is in good health so expects to live until he retires at age 65. He can get a 13 percent annual rate of return from utility stocks, bonds and a high income mutual fund. If he cashes in the policy, that $6,000 will grow, with prompt reinvestment for compounding, to $10,000 in less than five years. He will be ahead of the game unless he dies in the near future!

And if he needs extra money soon, he can cash in some of the investments rather than pay interest on a policy loan.

• If you own two whole life policies with equal death benefits, taken out at different ages, drop or cash in the newer one *unless* its annual premium is far less than that of the other. The dividends on the greater cash value of the older policy will be higher and thus can be used to reduce premiums or buy more coverage.

• If you own two policies taken out at about the same age, one with a mutual company and the other with a stock company, cash in the stock policy if it's over ten years old; the mutual one when it is under ten years old. The dividends paid by the mutual company will rise over the years and reduce your net cost.

N.B. With term insurance, where there's little or no cash value, the decision will be whether to drop or continue. The D-day will be when you reach age 65. At that time, term costs become comparable to those of straight life, which will pay dividends and build cash value. But be sure to determine whether payment of additional premiums will be worthwhile.

Other Benefits of Life Insurance

Borrowing. All straight life policies permit borrowing against the cash value. This provision is a handy way to boost income. Policies bought before January 1, 1978, permit loans with interest at 5 percent; those issued later, at 8 percent.

Thus, if you have an older $20,000 whole life policy with a cash value of $4,000, the loan from the insurance company will cost $200 a year. You invest the money in a money market fund that yields 12 percent so you get $480 and will be $280 a year ahead. Taxwise, the $200 interest is deductible against earned income, but the $480 will be taxable.

With a loan at 8 percent, the principle is the same but the benefits somewhat less.

Warning: The older you become, the more important it is to be cautious about borrowing. Any loan, based on life insurance, will decrease the value of your estate and thus the benefits for your heirs. Use such money only for safe, rewarding investments, not for speculations.

Estate Tax Savings. If the death proceeds of life insurance are payable to a specified beneficiary, there will be no estate taxes on these assets. Be careful: there must be no incidence of ownership, such as the right to change the beneficiary, cash or cancel the policy, borrow against cash value or retain a veto on the action of the beneficiary.

Life Insurance in Retirement Plans

In most cases, life insurance is not a suitable investment for pension plan funds. Contributions used to pay premiums for life insurance are not deductible with an IRA and only rarely with a Keogh Plan. They are deductible by a corporation, but the money used to pay premiums for life insurance must be included in the employee's gross income. Buying life insurance through a corporate pension plan makes sense only for high income earners. The details are complex so be sure that your insurance agent checks with experts in his company's home office and that you consult with your tax adviser.

To give you an idea of what's involved, here are examples digested from an article in *Physician's Management* as developed with Steven C. Glenn, CLU, manager of an agency of a major insurance firm.

How Not to Buy Life Insurance in a Pension Plan

Dr. G., a 45-year-old male, sets up a retirement plan under which the corporation buys a $100,000 straight life policy in combination with other investments.

The annual premium is $2,556. Under IRS rules (see table 9–5), the "cost" of the pure life insurance is $6.30 per $1,000. So Dr. G. must add $630 to his taxable income.

Over the years, the premium remains the same but the includable income rises: at age 50, the base is $9.22 per $1,000 so the taxable income is $922. In the 50 percent tax bracket, Dr. G. must earn $1,844 that year to meet this commitment (see table 9–6).

After retirement at age 65, Dr. G. can recapture, tax free, about $18,000. This is payable in a lump sum or in installments. He does get back his tax payments but loses the use of these savings for twenty years and has fewer dollars to invest for retirement income.

Effective Use of Life Insurance in Pension Plan

This example is typical of scores of options offered by insurance companies. It assumes that the participant wants to protect his family while working and seeks after-work income of 75 percent or more of his last working year's earnings.

The key investment is the annuity, not the life insurance.

Split-funded plan. This combines an annuity and a straight life policy. Dr. John J., aged 35, makes the maximum contribution through his professional corporation: 25 percent of his $100,000 annual earnings. He uses 60 percent ($15,000) to buy a flexible annuity (proceeds invested partially in common stocks), payable at age 65. With the other

Table 9–5.   IRS P. S. 58 Rates to Determine
Cost of Insurance

(One-year term premium for $1,000 life insurance)

Age	Premium
35	$ 3.21
40	4.42
45	6.30
50	9.22
55	13.74
60	20.73
65	31.51

NOTE: This is a summary; for full data, check IRS.

Table 9–6.   Buying Life Insurance through a Pension Plan

(Male, aged 45; $100,000 whole life; annual premium, $2,566)

Year	Death Proceeds	Additional Income Taxable Under P. S. 58
1	$100,355	$ 630
2	100,991	678
3	101,807	732
5	104,160	922
10	114,061	1,374
15	129,407	2,073
20	149,232	3,151

SOURCE: Steven C. Glenn, CLU, Jacksonville, Fla. 32207.

40 percent ($10,000), the corporation pays premiums on straight life insurance on Dr. J.'s life. Assuming the annuity yield is 9.75 percent and the insurance dividends are 6 percent, the death benefit grows rapidly: to $1,670,214 in twenty years and to almost $3.4 million in thirty years if Dr. J. works to age 65.

N.B. Neither rates of return are guaranteed and will vary over the years.

The corporation can deduct the full $25,000, but under P. S. 58, Dr. J. must include, as additional, fully taxable income, $1,314 in the first year; $789 in the second year, and, then, a gradually rising amount that will total $10,579 in the last working year (see table 9–7).

He will have the ever-greater protection for his family from the combination of the annuity and insurance: $667,950 at the outset; $1,227,706 in fifteen years; and a whopping $3,389,200 at age 65 when there are no more premiums. All accumulations are tax deferred.

At retirement, Dr. J. can count on a lifetime income of some

Table 9–7.   Split-funded Retirement Plan: Flexible Annuity Plus Life Insurance

(Male, aged 35; annual contribution 25% of earned Income of $100,000: $25,000 —60% used to buy flexible annuity; 40% to buy straight life insurance)

Year	Death Benefit: Straight Life Plus Annuity	Income Reportable Under P. S. 58
1	$ 667,950	$ 1,314
2	687,302	789
3	708,643	1,451
5	759,126	1,660
10	940,758	2,417
15	1,227,706	3,636
20	1,670,214	5,212
30	3,389,220	10,579

SOURCE: Steven C. Glenn, CLU, Jacksonville, Fla. 32207.

$250,000, and he can recover the extra tax payments without liability.

Section 162 Alternative

This combines an annuity with renewable term life under IRS Code Section 162. The death benefits remain the same: $667,950 but the premiums, even after using dividends to reduce payments, keep rising: from $1,226 in the first year to $2,288 in the tenth year and to $5,093 in the twentieth year. At this point, there are no more premiums because the cash value of the annuity, compounded at the assumed rate of 9.75 percent, will exceed the death benefit plus the value of the annuity (see table 9–8).

Again, the premiums are tax deductible by the corporation but must be included as income to Dr. J. Under Section 162, the imputed income (the official description of the amount of money taxed) will be about the same as under P. S. 58. But there is no recovery of taxes during retirement. Dr. J. accepts the fixed death benefit in return for no premium payments after age 55.

The best way to use life insurance in a corporate pension plan, says Steven Glenn, is with a 100 percent Flexible Annuity (FA). The corporation sends the annual $25,000 contribution to the insurance company which invests it in its annuity account. As shown in table 9–9, the assets grow at an astounding rate. At retirement, thirty years hence, Dr. J. will have $4,002,407—enough to assure a lifetime income more than quadruple his present income.

Table 9–8.   Combining Annuity and Term Life Insurance in Pension Plan

(Male, aged 35; fixed death benefit of $667,950)

Year	Premium	Dividends	Net Payment Under Section 162–Taxable Income
1	$1,226	$ 000	$1,226
2	1,279	000	1,279
3	1,353	675	678
5	2,288	788	1,500
10	3,403	1,115	2,288
15	5,240	1,757	3,483
20	8,186	3,093	5,093*

* No payments needed after 20th year because the annuity value exceeds the initial, static death benefit.

SOURCE: Steven C. Glenn, CLU, Jacksonville, Fla. 32207.

Table 9–9.   Buying 100% Flexible Annuity through Retirement Plan

(Male, aged 35; annual contribution 25% of earned income of $100,000, $25,000; interest rate 9.75%)

Year	Cash Value
1	$ 25,508
2	53,504
3	84,230
5	154,960
10	401,702
15	794,588
20	1,420,176
30	4,002,407

SOURCE: Steven C. Glenn, CLU, Jacksonville, Fla. 32207.

With the FA plan, Dr. J. must seek family protection outside his pension plan. Until about the eighteenth year, the cash value of the annuity will be less than the death benefit of the split-funded plan.

Older Individual

Now let's take a look at the pros and cons of life insurance in a pension plan for an older person. Dr. S., age 55, plans to work until age 70: 15 more years. He earns $100,000 a year and his corporation contributes 25 percent of his compensation to his retirement plan: $25,000.

There are many choices but let's settle on these:

• 100 percent flexible annuity(FA) with term life bought outside the plan with non-deductible, non-recapturable annual premiums of $2,296.

• Split funding (60 percent annuity, paid by the corporation) and 40 percent straight life (SF) purchased, by the corporation, outside the pension plan with tax deductible dollars which must be recaptured, by Dr. S., under P. S. 58.

At age 65, there is little difference (table 9–10) in the cash values of FA and SF: $401,702 and $324,103 respectively. But at age 70(when he plans to retire), the annuity, with compounding at 9.75 percent annually, is worth much more: $794,588 vs. $621,866.

With FA, Dr. S. always has $260,161 death benefit. With SF, this starts slightly higher, $276,613, but rises to $805,661 at age 70. To get this protection for his family, Dr. S. has to pay taxes on that portion of the annual contributions used to pay the insurance premiums: from $2,820 at age 55 to $4,960 at age 65. Notes Glenn, "That's not a great deal to pay for such security."

Dollarwise, Dr. S. would do better to use FA for his retirement income and buy the life insurance outside his pension plan. If he dies early, the added coverage will be worthwhile.

At some point, a decision will have to be made on how much and how long protection is needed. With his children grown, Dr. S. may feel safe with his annuity. But if he still wants to protect his widow, he can continue the insurance. Still, says Glenn, "At age 65, he can consider dropping the coverage with substantial annual savings."

Summary

When you buy life insurance through a pension plan, adds Glenn, you:

1. Choose safety over income. You protect your family against early death but you must accept a yield that is lower than available with alternative investments. In effect, you win only if you die young and buy a large amount of straight life insurance.

2. Commit yourself to the payment of higher taxes. While premium payments are deductible by the corporation, the P. S. 58 cost increases each year and becomes substantial when you are in your 50s and 60s.

The best plan is to purchase life insurance outside the corporate pension plan under Section 162. While part of the savings will be tax deductible, all of the contributions can be used to build retirement income. With no taxes, the fund assets will compound rapidly and will provide ample protection for the family while working and lifetime income in retirement.

Table 9-10.

Dr. S., aged 55: $100,000 compensation. Comparison of buying 100% flexible annuity (FA) with $260,616 term life bought outside with annual premium of $2,296, non-deductible and non-recapturable and split funding: 60% annuity bought with tax deductible dollars subject to recapture under P. S. 58. Current interest: 9.75%. Contribution: $25,000 annually.

	FA		60% FA	SF 40% Straight Life	
Year	Cash Value	Term Life	Net Premium	Cash Value	Death Benefit	Reportable P. S. 58
1	$ 25,508	$260,161	$2,296	$ 15,895	$276,613	$2,820
2	53,504	260,161	2,496	36,460	295,097	3,052
3	84,230	260,161	1,120	63,460	315,625	3,256
4	117,951	260,161	2,819	92,648	338,474	3,471
5	154,960	260,161	3,084	124,027	363,812	3,707
10	401,702	260,161	4,845	324,103	534,897	4,960
15	794,588	260,161	7,807	621,886	805,661	8,011

SOURCE: Steven C. Glenn, CLU, Jacksonville, Fla. 32207.

I realize that not many readers will be as affluent as the physicians, but these examples show why the purchase of life insurance through pension plans is seldom worthwhile . . . at any income level.

To repeat, life insurance is for family protection, not to build retirement benefits. The wisest course is to invest all pension plan contributions in order to build after-work income and to buy term life insurance with personal savings. If you start your pension plan fund early, save consistently, and invest wisely, the assets, at retirement, will assure enough income so that you will need only a modest amount of life insurance to cover final death expenses. You will be able to reduce your family protection and have more dollars to spend.

10. Don't Go Overboard with Health Insurance

Health is a major concern for everyone at all ages, but it is especially worrisome for retirees. When you work, you can count on monetary protection through sick leave and full or partial reimbursement of medical/hospital expenses as an employee benefit. After retirement, such coverage is seldom continued, but, at age 65, Medicare takes over. You should be glad it does because this can be the most important retirement benefit.

It is wise to have a basic supplementary policy, but there's no reason to go overboard with expensive coverage that is supposed to protect you against specific diseases or extraordinary health care costs.

In buying such a policy, take into account your own and your spouse's health history, your family financial situation and your personal sense of security. Then sign up only for coverage that you will logically need and that you can afford on your limited budget.

Still, if you and your spouse believe that there's likelihood of a serious illness when you are old, start a special fund while you are working. By saving just $100 a year and investing at a 12 percent rate of return, you will accumulate $8,070 in twenty years—after paying the taxes from other income or buying municipal bonds. That will pay for all but the most catastrophic illness. And the odds are still in your favor: 89 percent of all retirees never encounter severe medical expenses!

From personal observation and research, I am persuaded that there is no area of after-work living that is subject to more misrepresentation, uncalled-for fears and wasteful, often fraudulent, expenditures than health care. After age 65, medical/hospital expenses do rise about 50 percent to an average of 7 percent of total living costs, but a high percentage of these bills is covered by Medicare.

Once again, the problem is inflation. The government keeps raising the amount that must be paid by the retiree and the physicians and hospitals keep boosting their charges. In the past ten years, out-of-pocket payments, by the average Medicare beneficiary, have risen from $300 to $613 a year. In the next decade, they can be projected to double again.

Still, it seems to me, that, despite inflation, this is overly pessimistic because:

1. Medical care is becoming more capable of controlling many diseases/illnesses: overweight, high blood pressure, cholesterol, heart problems, arteriosclerosis, etc.

2. Hospital costs are being restrained, if not contained, by greater use of paramedics, nurse's aides, routine lab tests before hospital confinement, and expanded consumer/patient education.

3. There's hope that Congress will provide insurance against catastrophic health care costs, probably those above $3,500 per illness.

4. There are concerted, and successful, efforts to reduce costs and improve services at the family and community level.

True, the longer you live, the greater the chances of illness and the more severe it is likely to be. And, statistics show, more people are living beyond age 85. But, as my physician insists, old age accentuates, rather than causes, illness. The statistics are more fearsome than the facts.

Compared to the 45 to 64 age group, senior citizens spend almost twice as many days ill in bed, three times as many days in acute care hospitals and ten times as many days in nursing homes. By age 65, half of Americans have some sort of chronic ailment. "But," says my medical friend, "most of those problems have been around for some time. These 'ills' were not severe enough to interfere with work but now that they have little else to do, many retirees enjoy their suffering."

And, to prove his point, he adds these facts: 95 percent of retirees live outside institutions; 81 percent enjoy sufficient health to be able to move about independently; 83 percent were not in a hospital last year; and 89 percent never experience a severe, costly illness.

Take another look at that last figure because this is what scares most people: the overwhelming costs of a long, serious illness. But the truth is that only one of every eleven retirees is ever subject to extraordinary health care expenses and that 9 percent includes those who are already invalids or confined to institutions before age 65.

There is a close relationship between good health and financial security. The elderly widow, with inadequate income, is lonesome and depressed and a victim of poor nutrition. Her health will deteriorate rapidly. She needs special help.

Health Care Insurance

For those over age 65, there are two types of publicly administered health care insurance plans:

Medicare, a broad federal program that covers everyone who is over age 65 and eligible for Social Security and certain disabled persons.

Medicaid, a supplementary federal/state program that provides special medical benefits for those with low incomes. Terms vary state by state, but in most cases, the benefits are limited, minimal and seldom applicable to those for whom this book is written.

To retirees, Medicare is the most valuable. For details, get a copy of *Your Medicare Handbook* at your local Social Security office. Here are the highlights, *at this time.* Coverage, costs and terms are changed frequently so get full information first.

The cost base, per individual, is $12.20 per month, usually deducted from the Social Security check. This is subject to annual adjustment to meet the rising costs of living.

Medicare has two parts: part A, hospital insurance; part B, medical insurance.

With part A, benefits start after you have paid the first $260 per period of illness. Then, it covers:

Hospital Care that is "reasonable and necessary" as determined by a committee of physicians. This includes costs of a semiprivate room, board, nursing, special care units, lab tests, X-ray and radiation therapy, casts and surgical dressings, splints and appliances, rehabilitation services and operating and recovery room expenses.

For inpatient care in a participating hospital (not all institutions are eligible) in each benefit period, Medicare pays for all covered services above that $260 for sixty days; all but $65 a day for the next thirty days; and all but $130 a day for sixty days additional lifetime reserve. Once used, those reserve days cannot be replaced. Care in a psychiatric hospital is limited to 190 inpatient days. (N.B. Watch for changes periodically.)

The first benefit period starts after the first time you enter a hospital after you receive Medicare protection. When you have been out of the hospital for sixty days, a new benefit period starts. There is no limit to the number of benefit periods.

Skilled Nursing Care in a facility certified by Medicare, is paid for all covered services for the first twenty days and for the next eighty days, all but $32.50 per day.

Home Health Services is unlimited when medically necessary, with Medicare picking up the full costs. Once you qualify, you can continue to receive benefits even if you need only occupational therapy.

With part B, Medicare pays for physician services, no matter where your doctor treats you, after a $75 deductible, and thereafter 80 percent of "allowed" charges. Generally, this covers costs of treatments, nursing, surgical services, X rays when part of treatment, transfusion of blood and drugs/biologicals that cannot be self-administered.

With outpatient surgery, Medicare pays 100 percent of the doctor's surgical charge if he accepts the amount approved by Medicare as the full charge. BUT, often, the physician will levy an additional fee which becomes your responsibility.

There are limits to special treatments: i.e., for outpatient physical therapy, $500 annually; for psychiatric care, $250 a year.

Medicare does *not* cover: custodial care; routine physical checkups; hearing and eyeglass examinations; drugs and medicines you buy; most dental care; eyeglasses; hearing aids; routine foot care; dentures; orthopedic shoes; private duty nurses; homemaker services; personal conveniences such as TV and telephone while in the hospital; and acupuncture.

Again, check first because, with the financial pressures that beset Social Security, some terms are likely to be revised.

And *one timely note:* be sure to enroll in Medicare three months before your sixty-fifth birthday. Otherwise, you won't be eligible until the following January and won't be covered until July that year.

Getting the Most from Medicare

To assure the full benefits of this health care insurance, keep accurate records of all medical charges and special health care services. Fill out the proper forms and send them in periodically, preferably each time expenses (over that deductible which you pay) but always at the end of the calendar year. Medicare starts anew each January.

Medicare is complex. Its coverage is limited, but it does pay for most major expenses; its forms can be puzzling; and only a few physicians will handle all details. In most cases, you are responsible for the paperwork. Still, Medicare is one of the most valuable financial aids for retirees. Use it wisely; read the regulations carefully; try to follow directions; and don't be afraid to ask for help: from a community service agency or your local Social Security office.

Supplementary Insurance

There is still need for insurance to supplement Medicare: to pay for the deductibles and over-Medicare costs. In most cases, one policy should be enough and should not cost more than $400 a year for both husband and wife. If you want broader coverage, analyze each policy carefully to avoid duplication and unnecessary protection.

The best place to start is with the insurance you already have. There will be no waiting period after you're 65, and the cost will probably be less than that of a new policy. If you're lucky, your employer will continue to pay the premiums for a few years.

When you have to buy your own, shop around and get information from companies that specialize in retirement insurance. Generally, their rates are competitive, their coverage adequate, and their service good because they are familiar with costs and services not covered by Medicare. N.B. To reduce the federal deficit, Congress will shift more costs to the individual, so supplementary insurance will be more inportant in the years ahead.

Checkpoints for Supplementary Health Insurance

Does the policy:

- Pay all or part of the deductible that the individual must pay before Medicare starts covering the first 60 days in a hospital?
- Pay the per diem cost that Medicare doesn't cover when your hospital stay runs between 61 and 90 days?
- Pay the per diem charges that Medicare doesn't cover when you stay in the hospital more than 90 days and must use some of your lifetime reserve days?
- Provide coverage after the 150 days in a hospital that are fully or partially paid by Medicare?
- Pay for inpatient costs in a psychiatric hospital after 190 days available under Medicare?
- Help pay medical costs above the $75 deductible and any part of the costs above the 80 percent Medicare-allowed charges?
- Pay anything if you have to stay in a skilled nursing facility for over 100 days?

• Pay for the hospital costs after you have paid the deductible per each spell of illness?

• Pay all or part of the costs above $250 annually allowed for outpatient psychiatric services paid by Medicare?

• Make any provision for payment of non-Medicare expenses such as private nursing, routine dental care, eyeglasses, hearing aids, dentures, long-term custodial care in a nursing home or medical care in a foreign country?

For a guide, send $1 to Senior Information and Referral Center, P.O. Box 3582, Chico, CA 95927.

Six months before retirement, review all health care insurance: the company plan with the personnel department; your own policy with your agent or the local Blue Cross/Blue Shield representative. Take time to understand these provisions:

Key definitions. Such terms as "preexisting" conditions generally refer to all illness/symptoms you may have had before buying the policy. All too often, this can eliminate payments for the most expensive illnesses.

Waiting period. This should be no more than sixty days. You want immediate protection and should not have to wait two years before you can collect.

Duplication. Most policies will not reimburse you for costs already reimbursable through other protection. Do not be taken in by a glib salesman who implies that you can make money if you have several policies. One 87-year-old woman paid $4,000 for nineteen different policies written by nine different companies. They were largely worthless because of duplication. If your policy sets specific payments for specific costs and the company is reputable, that's all you need.

Extended hospital stays. Usually, this refers to payment of all hospital bills *after* ninety days (the maximum coverage of Medicare). This is not only very expensive but, practically, wasteful. Only .03 percent of all hospitalized retirees are confined that long. Those who continue to be confined to bed will be moved to a nursing home where they will be eligible for Medicare.

Hospital indemnity insurance. This pays a fixed amount, typically $20 to $50 for each day a person is hospitalized regardless of the actual charges or other insurance. Since most hospital stays are short-term and adequately covered by Medicare, you are, in effect, buying a possible cash bonus. Since premiums average about $175 a year, you will have to decide whether such an outlay is worthwhile.

Policy payout limits. This refers to the maximum payment. A lifetime limit is not good because it seldom provides adequate protection for a series of accidents/illnesses. The best policy is one that has a "per cause" maximum. Thus, if your benefits for a stroke are exhausted, you would still be protected for the costs of a broken hip.

Renewability. This should be guaranteed and should provide that premiums can be raised only for a group/class and not for an individual policyholder. Watch out for policies, especially those sold through the mail, that headline "lowest premiums." This can be a come-on. On renewal, there may be a sharp increase.

Special Illness Policies

Whether you are working or retired, avoid special illness insurance: for cancer, heart disease, etc. According to the House Select Committee on Aging, the elderly spend $1 billion a year on worthless, unnecessary health care insurance because salesmen "exploit fear for profit": a 50 percent commission on new policies and 10 percent on renewals.

Testimony revealed these exaggerations with cancer policies:

Claim: 1 in every 4 people is a victim of cancer.
Fact: 1 in 280 people gets cancer and that includes many whose cancers are not severe or costly.

Claim: The average bill for long-term cancer illness is $40,000.
Fact: The average cost is $10,000 and that includes many expenses that would occur anyway.

Claim: Our policy pays hospital benefits for stays over fifty days.
Fact: Only 1 percent of all cancer victims are confined anywhere near that long.

Claim: We pay benefits of $250,000.
Fact: The average payout is less than $1,000.

The Committee also pointed out that cancer insurance returns less than 50 percent of the premium to the policyholder while standard health insurance policies, such as Blue Cross/Blue Shield, pay back 90 percent of their premium income.

For information and assistance on health care insurance, contact the insurance commissioner in your state or the Bureau of Consumer Protection, Federal Trade Commission, Washington, D.C. 20580.

Saving Money with Hospitals

One of the most effective ways to cut health care costs (especially after retirement when you have more time) is to shop for a hospital. This may not please your physician but, in many cases, he/she is affiliated with several institutions so should not object too much.

Do select the hospital, on your physician's list, that: (1) accepts Medicare; (2) will prepare forms and send bills directly to the state Medicare office; and (3) has the best facilities for specific types of ailments/illness.

Don't go into a hospital on Friday. Studies show that these late-in-the-week admissions result in longer stays because (1) the hospital is not fully staffed on week-ends; (2) you'll have to wait until Monday morning before all the necessary laboratory and other diagnostic tests can be performed. Meantime, you'll be paying (with Medicare's help) $200, or more, for your "hotel" room.

Do try to enter the hospital on Tuesday. These stays are the shortest. By cutting the hospital confinement by just one day, you can save up to 25 percent of your costs.

Do ask your physician to have some of the routine lab tests done before you're admitted to the hospital. Most Blue Cross plans pay for these preadmission testing programs.

Don't feel you must have complete privacy. Take a semiprivate room. The costs will be less, and you'll leave more space for others.

IV.

FINANCIAL PLANNING
AFTER RETIREMENT

After work, financial planning is more important and easier than while you were tied down to a job. Unless you have ample resources, your more-or-less fixed income will be squeezed by inflation and you may, and probably will, need to make maximum use of all of your assets.

Planning should not be difficult if you set your mind to it. You are in a better position to control your expenditures because there will be ever-fewer business, community and social pressures and, if you move to a new area, you can set your own pace.

You will also have more time to take steps to offset the impact of inflation by planning shopping and vacations, doing your own repairs, making your investments more rewarding, turning illiquid assets into cash, and taking advantage of money-saving opportunities. Also, with the realization that your life span is shortening, you can plan to make the best use of the future and assure an orderly transfer of your estate after your death.

In all planning, be realistic but not penurious. You worked hard to get enough money to retire. Spend it wisely for your own personal pleasure, and, at some point, do not be afraid to draw on capital. That's what you saved for! The older you grow, the more you will realize the importance of that phrase "You can't take it with you."

11. What to Do When You Need Extra Money

No matter how carefully you plan or how ample you think your reserves after retirement, there may come a time when you will need extra money, usually for an emergency but, occasionally, permanently. *Do not panic.* You have weathered such problems before and, for retirees, there are numerous places to turn for help and many steps that can be easily taken.

Cash emergencies can result from a lost, stolen, or disputed check or nonpayment of a debt due. Credit crises will probably be unexpected: heavy expenses for a new roof, air conditioner, car repairs or medical bills or if you haven't been alert, from investment losses.

Lack of adequate income will be sparked by (and usually blamed on) inflation, but in many cases, it will reflect poor planning. With few exceptions, the long-term need for additional money will be more disturbing mentally than financially. Some folks may be living beyond their means, but most are not taking full advantage of all of their assets.

It's not easy to change lifestyle, but if the choice is between eating regularly and pride, there's only one logical answer—as difficult as such a decision may be.

What to Do

1. *Break the problem down into its component parts:* try to discover what happened, why it happened, how much money you really need and when.

2. *Refer to your net worth:* review all assets to determine which ones can be utilized for the biggest and quickest benefit with the least detriment to the future.

3. *Check your bills:* just because you have always paid accounts on time, there is no reason why you must continue such a laudable policy.

Almost all creditors are willing to wait when they have assurance of ultimate payment.

4. *List your debts in order of importance:* for the mortgage, utilities, department stores, physician, and so on. Call the bank or store credit manager, explain your situation and suggest new deadlines that you feel you can meet. If you see no immediate solution, make an appointment to get suggestions from these experts. They will probably be sympathetic, especially when you dress in old clothes and scuffed shoes. You may have to pay penalties, in extra interest or fees, but you'll have that important peace of mind.

5. *Set up warning procedures:* avoid a recurrence of such financial problems.

Whatever you do, remember that, in retirement, it will be difficult to run away, and there will be limited opportunities for new sources of income. Keep your cool. As one credit counselor told me, "Ninety percent of money problems of retirees can be worked out when both parties cooperate."

Once you have eased the immediate pressure, start to put your finances in order, first by economizing, then by utilizing your assets.

• Reduce all expenses, first selectively and then arbitrarily, by an across-the-board cut of, say, 10 percent.

• Postpone planned expenditures: for new clothes, a trip to see the grandchildren and all outside entertainment.

• Find substitutes for nonessentials. Instead of that before-dinner martini, drink seltzer with a lemon peel. After a couple of weeks of discipline, you'll hardly know the difference!

• Reevaluate your total budget. You'll be surprised at how long you can make do or do without if you set your mind to it. Those of you who lived through the Great Depression know what I mean.

The time will come when you're ready to start spending, but, with discipline and determination, you'll get by for a couple of months, which should be long enough to get those bills under control.

Getting Cash and Income

From a review of your net worth, list your assets in order of liquidity and value. Then, number each major item according to its *real* financial importance. You are facing a crisis which has little room for tradition or sentiment. You may have to sell low or nonincome-producing assets, such as growth stocks; real estate held for appreciation; household and personal items that have not been used in the last five years.

With large objects, such as grandma's dresser or that carved bookcase, find a reputable local dealer. With smaller items, divide them into two groups: (1) valuables such as jewelry, paintings, dolls, electric trains, etc.; (2) bric-a-brac, books, sporting goods, kitchen utensils, china and, when in good condition, clothes.

You can pick up money fast with jewelry and, by phoning dealers listed in the Yellow Pages, can get leads on the sale, directly or by consignment, for the other items. With the second group, your best bet will be a garage sale or a table at a flea market or similar mart. You may have to sit all day, but the results can be worthwhile and you'll meet some interesting people. But remember, you came to *sell,* not to *buy.*

These tactics can be continued after the financial crunch has passed. Each year, at an antique show in her church, my sister displays several of her old dolls and doll furniture. In each of the last three years, she's received over $500 which, fortunately, she has been able to donate to the church. But for some folks, such a sale may be the difference between fear and serenity.

It's never easy to part with once-cherished possessions, but they are not bringing in money and, after you and your spouse are gone, they will probably be sold for pennies to some unknown secondhand dealer. You need the cash NOW.

Don't be afraid to borrow:

• Against the cash value of your whole life insurance. The interest rates of such loans are low: 5 percent for National Service Life policies; 6 percent to 8 percent for regular policies. When you arrange such a loan, be realistic and recognize that this debt is not likely to be repaid so that your estate will be reduced by the amount of the debt. All it means is that there will be less to leave to your heirs.

• From a commercial bank with an insurance policy or securities as collateral. The interest rate will be high—currently up to 20 percent—and you'll have to make regular repayments, but you'll sleep better.

• From a thrift institution with your savings account/certificate of deposit as security. The loan can be up to 90 percent, will carry an interest rate higher than that received from the savings and, when a CD is involved, will mature at the same date.

• Against the value of your home: by a mortgage, refinancing, or a second mortgage. These are not quite last resorts but are close to them. Such loans are costly and can be burdensome in the future.

If the house is free and clear, a mortgage will be easy. If there's already a loan, refinancing can provide cash but will require bigger monthly payments because of the much higher interest rate. A fifteen-year mortgage (the usual maximum for retirees), at 16.5 percent will cost $18.05 per $1,000 compared to $13.27 at 10.5 percent.

A second mortgage will depend on your equity (the difference between the worth of your property and the balance due on the first mortgage). It will be expensive—about 3 percent higher than the interest rate paid on a primary loan; will be short-term, five to ten years; and, probably, will necessitate a large final balloon payment. But you will be putting an unused asset to work and will get money enough to pay your bills and set up a modest savings account, too.

In some areas, it may be possible to arrange a reverse mortgage. This is like a sale and lease-back (see chap. 18). It's not cheap and is really worthwhile only if the value of your home can be expected to continue to appreciate and your life spans are relatively short.

Cash in some of your whole life insurance. The older you are, the wiser this step can be, even when there is no emergency need for the money. With long-held policies, the cash value will be close to, or with accumulated dividends, more than the face value. For the past few years, most of that cash value has been your money and has been earning only a modest return.

By cashing in an older policy, you can get quick cash and what's left after paying your bills, can be invested at a welcome rate of return. Again, it's the old story of making maximum use of your assets.

Sell your home to your son or daughter. Do this only if family relations are good, you can get cash enough to meet the crisis and you and your spouse have the right to remain in the home as long as you want or, possibly, live.

This should be a business deal with formal documents and financing arrangements that are reasonable for both parties and acceptable to IRS.

Invade capital by selling securities or real estate. This is repeated because it is a tactic that is hard for most of us to accept. We spend working years trying to accumulate money and to invest it for rewarding returns. Suddenly, we have to think about reversing this habit. This is a decision that must be made by logic, not emotion, and for older folks, that's not easy.

Once you are really retired, there's no necessity to build a large estate. Presumably, your children are self-supporting, making more money than you ever did, and not in need of a large inheritance. It's your money to use constructively, to lessen current stress, and to make the rest of your life more comfortable. You can't take it with you. With the present high yields on investments, most people can withdraw 15 percent of their capital annually for longer than their own, or spouse's, actuarial life (see table 11–1).

Table 11–1.   How Long Assets Will Last When You Draw on Capital

Annual Yield	Number of Years/Months at This Rate of Annual Withdrawal			
	12%	13%	14%	15%
10%	18.7	15.1	12.10	11.2
11	24.4	17.9	14.5	12.4
12	Forever	23.2	17.0	13.11
13	Forever		22.3	16.4
14	Forever			21.4
15	Forever			

SOURCE: C. Colburn Hardy, *Funk & Wagnalls' Personal Money Management*, New York, N.Y., 1977.

Example: Chuck and Sophie W., both 70 years old, find that their expenses are outpacing their largely fixed income. They have $30,000 in savings certificates and $50,000 in a mix of common stocks with dividends averaging 8 percent annually.

They want to fix up their home, replace their car and travel more. But not all at the same time. They project these extras at $3,500 a year. For safety, they keep their savings, sell their $50,000 in stocks and buy shares of a no-load, income-oriented mutual fund yielding over 12 percent.

They arrange to take out 15 percent of their fund investment each year. This will provide the extra money annually for a little less than fourteen years—well above the actuarial life of Chuck and a bit less than that of Sophie. They still have $30,000 for emergencies and to replace the Social Security income that will be reduced by Chuck's death.

Or he could use the proceeds to buy preferred stocks or long-term bonds yielding about 14 percent. There would be more income, but they would have to space their expenditures as the checks would come quarterly for the preferreds and semiannually for the bonds.

Caution: Be slow to make this decision, but not too slow. You may not be able to reap the benefits if either or both die early. And do not withdraw a large sum at the outset because this will leave less money to earn income. Plan ahead. If you're worried about too fast depletion of capital, set a lower withdrawal rate that will provide less money for a longer period. You can always boost the payouts.

Some of these suggestions apply to emergencies, but most of them are suitable for both quick and long-term needs. But remember that when you are retired, the capital you spend, for any purpose, is gone and is not likely to be replaced.

If your goal is a happy, financially secure retirement, use your assets for emergencies, when necessary; for pleasure while you are both well and active. That's what the money was saved for in the first place.

Second Career

Obviously, one solution for extra money is for one or both of you to work. Under new rules, full Social Security will be paid when annual earnings, for retirees, aged 65 or over, are no more than $6,000. Above that figure, there's a reduction of $1 in benefits for every $2 in earnings until age 70 when there are no penalties. If you need income, look for the most remunerative opportunity, but be sure to calculate your net income if you earn more than the limit set by Social Security.

If you can afford to be choosy, cater to your own abilities and interests. That's one of the joys of retirement. In almost every community, there will be part-time positions: clerking in stores on weekends, holidays or as a vacation fill-in; preparing tax returns if you are financially savvy; repairing appliances; or selling insurance, real estate or products with which you are familiar.

Don't take the first job offer. Take a businesslike approach by getting in touch with people who make decisions on hiring: through ads, employment agencies and friends. Send out a score of resumes to prospects. They don't get people jobs but they can set up an interview when you follow up vigorously.

Do not be afraid to start a new career if you feel you have unique interests or skills: as a reporter on the local newspaper or radio station if you like to write; as a photographer if picture-taking has been your hobby; as a cooking teacher or caterer if you, or your spouse, enjoy working in the kitchen.

You can start planning before you retire, often with help from your employer. IBM, for example, has a Retirement Education Assistance program that provides potential retirees and spouses with $2,500 each in tuition aid for three years before and two years after work. This money can be used to attend local colleges that offer a variety of courses: jewelry making, motor repairs, ceramics, crafts, entrepreneurship for those who want to start their own business.

Unless you have ample assets, go slow in any second career that requires a substantial investment. Most new enterprises lose money for the first year or two and if you face severe competition or become ill, you may lose money that cannot be replaced.

On the other hand, don't be timid. Even if you don't make as much as you anticipate, you can have fun and the satisfaction of doing something you've always dreamed of. To many Americans, a second career can combine the best elements of retirement and full-time employment.

Other Benefits

There are also a number of special programs to provide financial aid/training/work services for older people. Generally, they are designed for those with limited incomes but if you need help, find out about them from your local Office of Aging. That's what these agencies are there for.

There are all sorts of special deals for old folks: discounts for car rentals, motels, restaurants, entertainment and prescription drugs; low-cost health exams; special transportation, such as buses to medical centers; senior citizen centers for recreation, education, training, and cultural activities; and cut rates for fishing and hunting licenses, bus fares, and so on. By taking advantage of these services, you can ease your budget pains. And you'll probably make some new friends.

For veterans (ninety days of service in the U. S. Armed Forces and a discharge under conditions other than dishonorable), there are a variety of financial aids: guarantees for home mortgages and, if your income is limited, pension payments and health services.

Veterans Administration hospitals give preference to servicemen and women who received disability for injuries or disease incurred or aggravated in the line of duty, but all veterans are eligible when there are facilities and funds available. A qualified veteran can get emergency care at any time; hospitalization or nursing home care when there are beds; and, if you are willing to wait your turn, outpatient medical, alcohol, and drug treatment through a VA hospital. For information, check the nearest VA office or the local American Legion Post.

Summary

In America, no one need go hungry or lack basic medical care. We may be slow in developing protective programs, but as a nation, we do care, and we do try to provide help for senior citizens.

There may be problems of misunderstanding, eligibility, and delay, but if you really need help, do not hesitate to ask for assistance and information from your local Social Security office, welfare department or community service agency.

Remember: most retirees are worth more than they think. When there are needs for extra money, it's usually more a question of how to use the resources you have than of finding outside help.

12. Problems and Solutions of Singles and Women

Single people, whether unmarried, divorced, or widowed, have special problems in both retirement planning and retirement living. Their financial needs may be less, but in many cases, their taxes are greater, their resources are more limited and their benefits smaller than those of married persons. They need financial planning to protect themselves while working and to assure those financially secure after-work years. Yet too few singles develop an effective program. As a result, at retirement, their incomes are meager, and at death, their estates are, to say the least, confused. And too many married women forget that the odds are that their husbands will die first and they will be widows for many years.

This chapter concentrates on single women because, compared to men, there are more of them, they live longer, and their incomes, while working and after retirement, are likely to be less. Yet, many of the following caveats and suggestions are applicable to both sexes.

At this time, the statistics are distressing, but as more women work at better wages and salaries, receive better pensions, and take advantage of IRAs, the situation will improve. And well it should: by age 65, the average woman, if married, has spent more than half her adult life as a member of the paid labor force; if unmarried, she has worked forty-five years, three years longer than the average male.

There are 10 million American widows: 9 of every 10 women will be widowed at some time in their lives; at age 60, only 50 percent are living with their husband; two out of every five marriages end in divorce; only 25 percent of retired women receive pensions and just over 2 percent of elderly widows receive benefits from their husband's private/government pension. In most cases, fortunately, the situation can be expected to improve. At least, there are new opportunities and, hopefully, more protective legislation.

Child Benefits

Social Security still pays benefits for children when the primary wage earner is retired, disabled or deceased. These benefits are based on what is known as the primary insurance amount (PIA). This is calculated on the record of the primary wage earner and provides over $100 per month, depending on the number of children under age 18.

For the child, age 18 to 21 attending college, the payments are dwindling and will be phased out in 1985.

Widow's Benefits

When there are no dependent children, the widow's benefit, from Social Security, is related to her age and the amount her deceased husband would have been entitled to or was receiving when he died: from 71½ percent at age 60 to 100 percent at age 65. But if she has been working and paying Social Security taxes, she will get her own benefit if it is higher than that of her husband.

A young widow who remarries will lose Social Security but one who remarries after age 60 will not be penalized. She will still get her former husband's benefits, but she can take a wife's benefits based on payments to the new husband, if they are larger.

• A woman, aged 62 or older, divorced after ten years of marriage, gets benefits when her ex-husband dies or starts collecting Social Security.

• A divorced woman, 60 or older (50 if disabled), who has been married for ten years or has young children, may be entitled to a widow's benefits even if the ex-husband remarries and his new wife gets Social Security benefits.

N.B. Single men get benefits, too: a widower can draw Social Security based on his wife's account if he was dependent on her for half of his support during the last years of his life. A widower with children is also entitled to benefits under the formulas outlined above.

For full details of these and other related payments, ask your Social Security office for *A Woman's Guide to Social Security* and *What Women Should Know about Social Security*.

Recognizing the inequities of the Social Security system, the 1981 White House Conference on Aging (WHCA) made a number of recommendations to provide more equitable treatment of widows and divorcees.

Among these were recommendations that:

• Veterans benefits for widows and children be restored

• Credit for Social Security be given in quarters of those years devoted to child bearing and child rearing

• Head of household classification, for income tax purposes, be established for widows and divorcees

• All annuity options must be signed by both husband and wife (so that employer pensions will continue after death of primary wage earner)

Pension Benefits

The biggest shock for most widows occurs after the death of the retired husband. When there are no dependents, her income will be cut sharply. She will receive only two-thirds of the Social Security previously paid because the check will not include her 50 percent extra, and, in most cases, she can no longer count on that government/private pension. It's sad but true that some 90 percent of men, eager for the highest retirement benefits, arrange for their pension to be paid only for as long as they live.

Example: Jack and Jill K., both retired, have been receiving $16,000 a year: $6,000 primary Social Security; $3,000 for the wife; $5,000 from a corporate pension and $2,000 from investments. When Mr. K. dies, her income is cut to $8,000: $6,000 Social Security and $2,000 from investments.

To avoid this often-disastrous situation, the WHCA recommended that legislation be enacted to require that both spouses must agree before survivor benefits are rejected. This will mean smaller monthly payments but will provide lifelong protection for both partners. And for future retirees who take advantage of the new IRAs, there will always be pension income because the assets go to the widow tax free when she is named as beneficiary.

Financial Planning

At any age, and certainly well before retirement, every person should see a lawyer about three things: a will, power of attorney and, when assets are substantial, a trust.

• The will allocates the estate as you wish, not by impersonal court action.

• The power of attorney, assigned to a relative, friend or attorney, will assure that someone takes over if you become ill or disabled and will pay bills, deposit checks and act on important matters such as a lease, investments, etc.

• A trust will protect assets while living and, at death, will avoid probate costs and fees for estate appraisal and thus reduce legal expenses. As explained in chapter 14, a revocable trust will remove income from your tax return, and return it for future use. By arranging for an outside trustee, the assets will be protected if you should become incapacitated. When you are young and healthy, it's difficult to be concerned about illness, disability, or death. But none of these actions cost much and all of them become increasingly important as you accumulate wealth and grow older.

If you have substantial assets, you may want to set up trusts for your estate. In most cases, however, this will not be necessary because of the tax breaks under the 1981 Economic Recovery Tax Act.

It's also wise for singles to have a modest amount of life insurance (especially when not part of employee benefits) to pay for estate administration charges and taxes (more likely to be state than federal), to provide funds for gifts to relatives and bequests to college or charities. Just because you are single and have no direct financial responsibilities to others is no reason why your assets should not be properly protected and distributed as you want.

This type of planning is especially important for divorcees. In community property states, a divorced spouse has the right to share in pension assets. In other states, the laws vary widely. In Colorado and Missouri, the divorced party has no interest in the unvested interest in a pension plan; in others, there are legal distinctions between vested and unvested retirement assets. Make sure that these questions are discussed by both attorneys at the time of a formal separation agreement.

In Florida, for example, many elderly widows and widowers set up trusts with the local bank as trustee. This makes certain that someone will be responsible if they become ill or incapacitated. Do this only when you have ample assets as the administration/maintenance fees can become expensive.

For most people, planning for widowhood is difficult and distasteful. Ideally, it should start early and involve both husband and wife: in budgeting, in calculating net worth, in making investments, in projecting future assets and after-retirement needs and in being fully informed about income. There are few things sadder and more difficult to straighten out than a spouse who has no knowledge of family assets, liabilities or financial responsibilities.

The first time a husband and wife discuss the when, whether and how of retirement, the wife should plan to take these steps:

• Set up her own bank account and pay her bills with her personal checks. A joint account may be all right for checking and savings accounts but, at death, the funds may be impounded, uncashed checks in the deceased's name must be held and important bills will not be paid. To arrange for both partners to draw on each other's personal account, as the bank for special power of attorney form.

• Establish her own credit: with retail stores, gasoline companies, credit card firms, etc. Despite federal regulations, it is still difficult for single women who are not working and do not have direct references to establish credit.

• Get to know family advisers: attorney, insurance agent, broker and accountant. Learn their areas of responsibility, methods of operations and charges and listen to their suggestions.

• Know the source and amount of all pensions and death benefits.

Most Common Mistakes

According to comments made at a local bar association panel, the most common mistakes of women that lead to trouble when they are widows or divorcees are these:

Short-sightedness in career planning. Accepting a job as a typist or clerk in hopes of meeting men rather than using it as a stepping stone to a more responsible position; unwillingness to keep up special skills while raising a family; reluctance to accept part-time work when single because of social stigma.

These days, everyone who wants to work and has a little skill and a bit of gumption can find employment. The job may not be glamorous or high paying but it will bring in money, enable you to meet people and, hopefully, make friends. Even if you are well fixed, continue a career. It's more fun, more rewarding and more useful!

Being too conservative in investments. Maintaining a large savings account with a small (6 percent or less) yield when there are safe investments paying 12 percent to 15 percent annual rates of return (see chap. 8).

Reluctance to sell inherited assets. Jewelry, collections, furniture, art and heirlooms that are no longer used or cherished. If any item has not been displayed for five years or is not wanted by a relative, dispose of it while you are alive: by actual or designated gift to a relative or to an institution or by sale to provide money that can be used to pay for extra wants or needs.

"All too often," says a retired probate judge, "the executor of an estate lives thousands of miles away and has neither the time nor interest to make an inspection, let alone an appraisal. He hires a local lawyer who hires a local liquidator whose only interest is making as much money as fast as he can. From many years of experience, I am persuaded that the best policy for single people, especially with older women, is to Give While You Live."

Future Changes

Social Security was designed when most American women were lifelong homemakers who depended on their husbands for support. The retirement benefits were based on their status as dependents. With more than half of all women working today, the old rules/bases are no longer equitable and are being, and will be, changed. In a preliminary report, the President's Commission on Pension Policy points out a number of current inequities that discriminate against singles:

• If the spouse dies early, the survivor not only gets only 50 percent of Social Security but the benefits are computed on an outdated earnings base even though indexed for inflation.

• Two-thirds of a couple's Social Security benefits continue to the survivor of one-earner couples but only one-half when the spouse earned equal benefits. This is inequitable and creates financial hardships because the survivor will need more than 50 percent to maintain the previous standard of living.

• Most divorced women receive the low worker, not the higher spouse, benefit because they have been out of the labor force for many years. Unless the former wife receives alimony or other financial support from the ex-spouse, there is little logic as to why the spouse benefit should double when the ex-spouse dies.

The commission recommends that:

• Family earnings should be equally shared between spouses for Social Security credits

• The surviving spouse should inherit all or part of the deceased's wage record in marriage

• Pensions should be defined as property and taken into account at both divorce and survival and that survivors of employees who die before retirement with vested benefits should receive either survivor benefits under the pension plan or appropriate life insurance.

If these recommendations (which were, in general, approved by the White House Conference on Aging) are enacted, single persons, especially divorcees and widows, can look forward to better protection as they grow older.

Checklist for Wives—and Husbands, Too

• Make sure that both husband and wife have up-to-date wills. There were major changes in 1981 so every will should be reviewed with a lawyer to take advantage of the new tax savings.

• Know what, and where, your spouses's assets are. Is there a list of securities, real estate, etc.? Is it in a desk drawer, safe deposit box or with a broker? Do you know the amount of life insurance? the companies involved? the name and address of the agent?

• Before you sign any papers, read them carefully and understand what you are committing yourself to. This is especially important with income tax returns and contracts. You can be liable even though your spouse assures you that "it's routine."

• Take an interest in your spouse's business and all financial affairs. If you don't understand, ask questions and, as a last resort, consult an impartial, knowledgeable outsider.

• Keep originals or copies of all important documents—tax returns, insurance policies, deeds, wills, etc.—in a safe place.

• Know your spouse's professional advisers: lawyers, accountants, insurance agent, broker, investment manager.

• Get to know your spouse's trusted business associates—the people looked to for guidance.

• Make it a point to meet the bank/trust company official who will be responsible for acting as trustee or executor of your spouse's and your own will.

• Maintain your own bank account and credit cards.

• Use common sense in making financial decisions. If you do not feel comfortable with a decision or adviser, try to make a change.

13. Protecting Your Assets:
Wills, Executor, and Joint Tenancy

For those approaching or enjoying retirement, there is *nothing* more important than a will—for each partner. If you do not have such a last testament, or have not revised it lately, see a lawyer *immediately*. The 1981 Economic Recovery Tax Act made significant changes that make possible BIG tax savings (see chap. 14 on estate planning).

Simple wills require only a short visit to a lawyer and can cost as little as $150. Every adult in every family should have a will and should review it periodically to make changes to meet new laws and family situations.

If you die without a will, the state will provide one for you and, depending on where you live, the surviving spouse may get as little as one-third of what you intended. A court-appointed administrator will distribute your assets according to state laws which are always inflexible, usually impersonal and often contrary to your wishes. It is stupid to work a lifetime to build an estate and have most of your wealth apportioned by rote.

Despite this awesome prospect, *only half of all older Americans have wills and one-third of these documents will be contested because of poor drafting, errors, and angry heirs—all situations that can be easily and inexpensively avoided.*

The value of a will became even more important under the 1981 tax law. This eliminated the old tax-free maximum of $250,000 and permitted everyone to pass, tax free, an estate of any size to his/her spouse. With a properly structured will, by 1987, there should be no federal estate tax on any estate valued at $600,000 or less!

Consult a Lawyer

For general information about wills in the state where you live (or plan to live), get a folder from a bank or trust company and then consult an attorney, preferably with both spouses sitting in. He/she will show you how to protect your assets, save taxes, minimize settlement costs, set up trusts and assign rights for proceeds of life insurance and pensions. The small cost will be far more than offset by peace of mind from assurance that your loved ones will be protected.

Before you see the lawyer, be prepared with:

1. Clear ideas of what you want done with your assets

2. Complete information on your present and future wealth—property, life insurance, retirement benefits, and so forth

3. Up-to-date records on current values, dates and costs of acquisition and location of all valuables

Look at a will as a business venture because, for your heirs, this can be the key to their future well-being. Advanced preparation can save you money because while some lawyers have set fees for specific activities, most will charge by the hour. The better organized you are, the quicker the will can be drawn.

The attorney can be helpful with advice, but his primary role is as a legal technician who will prepare the document to meet legal requirements and to fulfill your wishes.

It may sound smart and economical to write your own will and to try to avoid probate (a court responsible for administration of estates of deceased persons), but, for anyone with even modest assets, this is foolish. A holographic (in your own handwriting) will is invalid in half of the states and, even then, must pass court scrutiny. And despite what some promoters aver, probate is neither difficult nor costly. Most legal requirements in our society are logical and useful, even though their procedures are not always efficient. The mistake you make today may not surface for ten or twenty years from now.

About Your Will

Your will is your last testament. It directs the disposition of your assets by a personal representative (executor), so it should be clear, specific and in conformity with laws and regulations. Any will can be challenged by heirs and/or relatives, but such a problem is less likely when the will is prepared by a professional.

Your lawyer will have suggestions and, probably, a sample form. The contents will vary according to wishes and wealth but, generally, should cover these areas:

1. Identify the maker by full name and principal residential address. This is essential when you have a vacation home in another state. Omissions could mean double taxation.

2. Name an executor: an individual or institution responsible for

carrying out your wishes, seeing that the will is probated, arranging for payment of debts and taxes and distributing assets as you state. If the executor is a lawyer or institution, the fees will be paid from the estate. You can save money by naming a relative or friend who may serve without remuneration but will probably retain legal counsel.

3. Provide enough income for your surviving partner. This should be in addition to her own cash, savings and checking account. There should always be sufficient funds, directly or through life insurance, to support the widow and, if dependent, children, until the estate can be settled. The lack of ready money can be tragic especially for a retiree who has no salary and limited personal assets.

4. Plan ahead for major expenses: for mortgage payments, educational bills if there are children and, especially for retirees, costs of the final illness.

5. Describe major gifts in detail. If you leave stock to a relative, specify that the number of shares should be adjusted to reflect splits, stock dividends, etc.: i.e., you give 100 shares of XYZ Corporation but, later this year, the stock is split three for one. Unless your wishes are spelled out, the relative will get only one-third of what you intended.

6. Make provision for distribution of bequests in the event that they cannot be made because of death or other changes: i.e., that the assets be given to someone else or become part of your residuary estate (what's left after other distributions have been made and taxes/expenses paid).

7. Be cautious about listing gifts of small items such as jewelry or personal possessions. Unless they are heirlooms, they may be sold or exchanged before you die. For such items, add a letter of instruction to the executor to specify distribution or, better, permit him to use his own judgment.

8. Make all monetary bequests in percentages, not dollars. If you specify "$10,000 to Yale University and $5,000 to St. Mary's Hospital," there may not be sufficient assets to make such gifts. It's wiser to state, "I bequeath 10 percent of my net estate to Yale and 5 percent to St. Mary's."

9. If you plan to disinherit some relative, be explicit: "After careful thought, I have concluded that it is better not to include a bequest to my cousin ———."

10. Do be specific, so that your lawyer understands exactly what you have in mind. One of my relatives owned a house on a 60-acre farm. In his will, he left "half the value of his home" to his cousin. The question, which ended in the court, was "Is the half value that of the

home alone or that of the total house and acreage?"

11. If your will was originally prepared before September 1981, add a codicil to change the wording to "unlimited marital deduction." Otherwise, the probate court may assume that you wanted your spouse to have only half the estate as specified under the old law.

12. Double-check the number of witnesses required in the state of residence. Some states mandate three signatures.

13. Keep the will up to date by revisions when situations change: when children become adults; when there's a divorce, remarriage or death of beneficiaries; when you move, sell or acquire property. A will drawn ten years ago is not likely to be pertinent today, especially when families are so mobile. Without revisions in your will, your estate could go to your divorced wife and/or her heirs.

14. When you make a new will, destroy the old one. Failure to do this can provide an opportunity for a disgruntled heir to start suit.

15. Insert a common disaster clause to cover the rare possibility of a joint death of you and your spouse.

16. Use proper legal names and addresses with charitable bequests. If you make a gift to the National Association for Chilblains and the real title is the Chilblain Association of America, there may be trouble if there's a rival organization with a similar name.

17. Review the will carefully to catch errors: in signatures, correct names of beneficiaries, description of properties, and so forth. If you signed your wife's will by mistake, it may be invalid.

Codicils/Instructions

Insofar as possible, keep the basic will intact and use:

• Codicils (supplementary comments and changes) for minor revisions such as naming a substitute executor, revoking or adding a bequest.

• Letter of instruction to your executor: to explain how you want to dispose of personal effects such as books, files, records, collections.

The Role of Executor

An executor, also called personal representative, is the individual or institution legally responsible for the management and disposition of an estate. The appointment is made by will and takes effect at death. If you die without a will, an executor will be appointed by a probate court.

An effective personal representative should be readily available and have some administrative skill and a lot of common sense. It is not a job for anyone who is unable or unwilling to be patient or to spend time with lawyers, heirs, and, on occasion, courts.

The executor has two responsibilities:

Legal: to identify and appraise the assets of the estate, to receive and invest income, to manage and/or sell property, to settle all debts and taxes, to make distributions according to the intentions of the deceased and to submit an accounting to the heirs and the court.

Personal: to provide solace and support to the survivors and to match the terms of the will with the needs and wants of the heirs. Ideally, the executor should have the humanity of a clergyman and the business acumen of a successful executive.

In most cases, the estate can be cleared up in nine months (the normal deadline for payment of federal taxes) but when there are inadequate records, special problems, such as a business or tax-sheltered investments, the settlement can drag out for years. And if the executor makes a costly mistake, the beneficiaries may have grounds for financial compensation.

Three Choices

In selecting a personal representative, there are three choices:

Institution: usually a bank or trust company. Such a choice will assure experience and continuity, but the administration may be impersonal and standardized and costs, for small estates, relatively expensive.

Before you designate an institution, discuss fees, philosophy and methods of operation. You can make a change while you live but, after death, such action must be approved by the court.

And do not be afraid to shop around. With thrift institutions moving into this field, service is being expanded and fees reduced.

Individual: typically a relative, family friend, business associate or lawyer. Personal attention can help your heirs, but when a nonprofessional is in charge, settlement can be slowed by the lack of experience or family squabbles. Always name a successor executor; if the original designee becomes ill or unavailable, removal can be embarrassing and will require court approval.

It's easy to name someone in your family but do not let sentiment override your judgment. . . . If your estate involves special assets such as real estate or tax shelters, think twice about naming your school-teacher son.

Don't overlook your spouse. If he or she has the ability to retain a competent lawyer, to follow well-established procedures and to make decisions, this choice may be the best.

Combination: this teams the personal touch of the individual with the experience of the professional. Both may get fees and, unless the duties are spelled out in the will, there may be hassles that can delay important decisions. This dual responsibility is best when the estate is large enough to require special expertise and when there are heirs who may be hard to locate.

Checkpoints

With older people, it's often more important to select empathy over skill. To many retirees, death is a crushing blow. The survivor needs understanding more than efficiency. And if there's a large family, there are likely to be squabbles and pressures that can best be handled by a tactful individual.

It's also important that the executor be available and have ready access to the courthouse because there will be numerous documents to sign. Postponements due to the absence of the executor can be costly to the estate, annoying to the heirs and inconvenient to the lawyer and the court.

Finally, look for someone who is at least five years younger than you are and in good health. After retirement, recheck every few years to be sure that the person is still willing and able to accept the responsibility. And do not hesitate to make a change if you, or your spouse, have any qualms. From personal experience, I can testify that an incompetent, or unwilling, executor can become a source of irritation and frustration.

Acting as an Executor

If you are asked to be an executor, be cautious, especially when you are retired. When the request comes from a younger relative, do not accept. The odds are that you will die first.

When the query comes from an older relative or friend, go slow. You may not outlive him, or, if you do, you may not be able to function effectively. If the will is to be probated at some distance, try to avoid the responsibility unless you can hope to stay with a relative. Transportation, food and lodging can be expensive.

If you feel you cannot refuse, ask for a coexecutor, preferably an institution or lawyer and start planning early by insisting on reading the will and discussing the provisions with the individual in the presence of an attorney. That's also good advice for the individual or institution you appoint as your executor.

Periodically, discuss specific actions that you want taken or, if you're to be the executor, that you will have to take: which stocks to sell first if money is needed? what lawyer to retain? and how and where to invest the proceeds of insurance policies?

Before retirement, a will and executor are important; after work, they are both essential.

The Role of a Trustee

A trustee is an individual or institution to whom trust property is legally committed. With single, small-sum trusts, any conscientious person can be named. With complex agreements involving large assets, the choice should take into consideration the special purpose of the trust, the types of property included and the scope of responsibilities. This is an area best served by a professional, such as a bank or trust company. Such a trustee is organized to provide a variety of services, submit annual reports, keep complete records and assure continuity. A compromise is to appoint cotrustees: your spouse with an institution or, when there are ample assets, a qualified investment adviser.

Usually, the individual, typically a relative or close friend, will serve with little or no remuneration, especially when there are provisions— and income enough—to retain professional counsel. An institution will charge fees based on a percentage of the value of the trust with a minimum seldom less than $500 a year.

In most cases, use the same checkpoints as suggested in naming an executor: someone who is not too old, in good health, available to the beneficiaries and with knowledge of your wishes.

Always consult a lawyer first and make provisions for: (1) a successor to be appointed by the beneficiary(ies), not yourself because there could be tax consequences; (2) removal of the trustee if administration or investment performance is poor; (3) regular reports and, if necessary, monitoring.

A trust involves fiduciary responsibilities which should be wisely and properly fulfilled.

Joint Tenancy

Joint ownership of property is convenient and does provide a sense of trust and security. But its use should be limited, preferably to modest bank accounts and, possibly, the home.

Historically, the major advantage of joint tenancy was that when one spouse died, the survivor, as coowner, inherited the property tax free, without probate or beneficiary designation. This automatic transfer took precedence over the provisions of the will of the deceased.

But, as the result of the 1981 tax law, joint ownership is no longer an easy way to avoid estate taxes. Starting in 1982:

1. Each spouse is considered to own half of the jointly owned property. Previously, ownership was based on whose money was used to acquire the assets.

2. There can be unlimited transfers of property from one spouse to the other—at any time and, usually, without tax consequences. Prior to the new legislation, to avoid paying estate taxes, it was smart to put life insurance policies in each other's name and to hold property, such as real estate, jointly. This is no longer necessary and seldom wise.

3. There are annual raises in the "unified credit" that can be applied against estate and gift taxes: from $225,000 in 1982 to $600,000 in 1987. For most people, this eliminated the need for trusts and other tax-avoiding devices.

4. The law established a stepped-up cost basis for property as of the date of death: i.e., securities acquired many years ago for $10,000 and now worth $50,000 are valued at $50,000 for estate tax purposes and for transfer to a beneficiary.

These changes diminish, if not eliminate, the traditional tax advantages of joint ownership. Since each spouse is considered to own half the property, the stepped-up cost basis applies to only 50 percent of the property ($25,000). If the value of these assets continues to appreciate, the estate taxes, at the death of the second partner, may be greater.

But if the first to die has sole ownership of the property, the survivor can inherit it tax free, and the cost basis of everything will be at the step-up, date of death value. Granted that most people will not have to pay estate taxes because their estate will be below the new limit, it's still worthwhile to see your lawyer and make certain that your will is in line with the law. Despite what some glib "experts" assert, joint ownership is never a substitute for a will.

Other Disadvantages of Joint Ownership

With all joint tenancy, there can be problems:

• If a couple has joint checking/savings accounts, either party can withdraw the money at any time without the permission or knowledge of the other. That means that if the marriage falters, one partner can take out all the money and move away. There is nothing that the other spouse can do about it!

N.B. If you prefer to have both partners have access to a bank account, arrange for a power of attorney for specific assets: for your wife on your personal checking account and for you on hers.

• A widow with children remarries and her property is transferred to a joint account with her new husband. If she dies, even with a will that states how the assets are to be distributed, the second spouse will get everything and there will be no inheritance for the children.

Joint ownership may have some mental benefits, but it is seldom a tax-wise decision. Joint ownership can create a false sense of security in that the individual neglects to establish financial independence. This becomes increasingly important after retirement when, like it or not, death draws closer. Each partner should have assets that can be used quickly and maintained safely. That's what planning is all about.

14. Estate Planning: Making It Easy for Your Heirs

As the result of the Economic Recovery Act of 1981, estate planning is a new ball game. In most cases, there is no longer need for trusts to shelter assets or to defer or to avoid taxes. Unless a married couple is relatively well-to-do (roughly a net worth of $300,000 today and $600,000 by 1987), there should be no federal taxes on the estate of the first to die. But there can still be substantial levies on the same assets at the death of the surviving spouse.

To be sure we're on the same wavelength, here's the definition of estate: The sum total of assets and liabilities of a decedent.

The new law provides for an unlimited marital deduction for both estates and gifts. There is no tax on assets transferred between spouses. The old marital deduction—the greater of $250,000 or half of the adjusted gross estate—has been eliminated. This negates trusts except under special situations: while working, to aid children/grandchildren and dependent relatives; after retirement, to make gifts and to save taxes for the surviving spouse.

Organizing Your Estate

To obtain the greatest benefits and to assure protection for your loved ones, it is still important to plan both estates: your own and that of your spouse. Here's what to do—with the aid of a lawyer:

Step 1: Prepare a master list of important documents and their location with the original attached to your will and copies for your lawyer, spouse and executor (see table 14–1). Be sure to keep this up to date.

Step 2: Determine your present and projected net worth. If you are still working, you will, presumably, grow wealthier as you grow older. If you are retired, you may be worth a bit less over the years because you will save only for specific expenditures, will be spending all or most

Table 14–1.   Checklist of Documents Needed for Estate Planning

Items	Location
Securities	
Corporate retirement plan	
Keogh or IRA plan	
Annuity contracts	
Stock-option plans	
Stock-purchase plans	
Profit-sharing plan	
Income and gift tax returns	
Title and deeds to real estate	
Title insurance	
Rental property records	
Mortgages/loan agreements	
List of valuables	
Auto ownership records	
Birth certificate	
Citizenship papers	
Adoption papers	
Military discharge papers	
Marriage certificate	
Children's birth certificates	
Divorce/separation records	
Names and addresses of relatives/friends	
List of professional and fraternal organizations	
Club membership certificate	
Other	
Will (original)	
Will (copy)	
Powers of attorney	
Burial instructions	
Cemetery plot deed	
Spouse's will (original)	
Spouse's will (copy)	
Spouse's burial instructions	
Special bequests	
Trust agreements	
Life insurance, group	
Life insurance, individual	
Other death benefits	
Property and casualty insurance	
Health insurance	
Homeowner's insurance	
Car insurance	
Employment contract	
Partnership agreements	
Checking/savings accounts	
Bank statements	

Table 14–1—*Continued*

List of credit cards
Certificates of deposit
Checkbooks
Savings passbooks
Brokerage account records

of your income and, in varying degrees, will be reducing your assets by gifts or invasion of capital. Moreover, when one partner dies, there will probably be less income because of a lower pension and Social Security benefits. But there may be greater assets resulting from payments of death benefits from life insurance (see table 14–2).

Table 14–2.   Calculating Net Worth: Before and After Retirement

Assets	While Working	After Retirement
Cash and equivalents	_____	_____
Savings accounts/CDs	_____	_____
Cash value, life insurance	_____	_____
Annuities, current value	_____	_____
Pension: vested interest	_____	_____
Securities/investments	_____	_____
Real estate	_____	_____
Home	_____	_____
Vacation cottage	_____	_____
Investments	_____	_____
Automobiles	_____	_____
Furniture/furnishings	_____	_____
Jewelry/furs	_____	_____
Collectibles	_____	_____
Other	_____	_____
Liabilities		
Bills payable	_____	_____
Mortgage balance	_____	_____
Credit cards payable	_____	_____
Loans	_____	_____
Taxes due	_____	_____
Pledges	_____	_____
Other	_____	_____
Net Worth:		
Assets minus liabilities	_____	_____

Step 3: Check your figures with table 14–3. This shows data for net worth for fear, comfort and joy. But watch out if most of these assets are not producing—or able to produce—income. These data can also be

used to determine when gifts can be made (discussed later in this chapter).

Table 14–3.   **Net Worth**

Age Group	Could Be Trouble	All Is Well	On Easy Street
40–49	$ 70,000	$150,000	$250,000
50–59	100,000	200,000	325,000
60–69	140,000	275,000	450,000

Step 4: With your attorney or tax adviser, project the tax consequences at the death of each spouse. Under the 1981 tax law, there's:

1. An increase in the "unified credit" that can be applied against estate and gift taxes (see table 14–4), so that federal estate taxes will be abolished for the majority of Americans. There can still be state inheritance taxes, which, in some areas, can be substantial.

Table 14–4.   **Size of Estate Exempt from Federal Taxes**

Year of Death	Unified Credit	Exempt Estate
1982	$ 62,800	$225,000
1983	79,300	275,000
1984	96,300	325,000
1985	121,800	400,000
1986	155,800	500,000
1987 and thereafter	192,800	600,000

Source: Internal Revenue Service.

2. Unlimited martial deduction. A husband or wife can give, or bequeath, all or part of his/her estate to the other spouse free of federal tax . . . at any time to any amount.

3. Increase in the annual, individual gift tax exclusion, from $3,000 to $10,000. Married taxpayers can jointly double the exclusion to gifts up to $20,000 with as many recipients as they like each year.

4. A new rule for timing gifts. Except for insurance policies going to children or their trusts, there are no time limits, thus eliminating the old provision that gifts made within three years of death were includable in the taxable estate of the deceased donor as being in contemplation of death.

Consult your attorney for details, but in most cases, it will be wise for the spouse who expects to die first, usually the older husband, to transfer most of the family's assets to the wife. This will increase the size of her estate but, as long as it is below the exempt limits, there will be no federal estate tax. If the total can be expected to be greater than those exemptions, taxes can be avoided when the husband transfers assets to his wife with a "qualified terminable interest" in the property. This is a form of trust that gives her the income from the assets for her life and, at her death, the principal to the heirs as the husband specifies. The will should state that the amount placed in trust for the children will equal the amount protected by the estate tax credit in the year of the husband's death and the remainder will go to a lifetime trust for the spouse.

Or, if the widow receives everything and that total is above the statutory limits, she can start making annual gifts. With two children and two grandchildren, she can give $40,000 a year. That's $200,000 in five years!

Trusts

While trusts are no longer as useful as in the past, they can be valuable under certain conditions. When you create a trust, you turn assets over to someone else to hold and manage for the benefit of a third party. Since you no longer control the assets, you and your estate can usually avoid paying taxes. But the most important consideration in setting up any kind of trust should be its purpose, not the tax benefits alone.

The key to a successful trust, in creation and management, is to know exactly what you want to accomplish, to be certain that the trustee understands your wishes and to be sure that the terms provide the benefits you want. Trusts can be used to:

• Provide income and, possibly, the principal for your spouse while living and the remainder, on death, to be held in trust for the children.

• Defer payment of income for life or a specific period of time.

• Circumvent probate and speed distribution of your estate.

• Keep your affairs confidential after your death.

• Bar a child from getting control of an inheritance at what you regard as too early an age.

• Prevent your widow from turning your hard-earned assets over to her new husband.

• Keep some assets out of the hands of creditors.

• Permit the retention of professional assistance.

Trusts can be described by these broad categories:

Living Trust. This continues as long as the beneficiary lives or for a set period of time. When the trust ends, the principal goes back to the original owner.

Testamentary Trust. This is created by will and takes effect only when the grantor dies. It is valuable in keeping holdings together so that they can be disposed of as you want and without losses that might result if a quick settlement has to be made and the executor has to liquidate the estate.

Revocable Trust. This may be terminated at any time during the lifetime of the creator. It can hold property that will revert to the donor when the trust is terminated and thus becomes subject to taxes on income earned by the trustee and, at death, on the full assets. It is useful primarily to permit the owner to look at how his estate plan will operate. If anything is unsatisfactory, the trust can be amended, altered or dissolved.

Example: Lou R., a busy lawyer, has $100,000 that he plans to leave to his handicapped daughter. He wants to be sure she is cared for with concern and efficiency and will always have adequate income. He sets up a trust with a local bank. After three years, he decides that his daughter can handle her own affairs so dissolves the trust.

It can also be useful for retirees who continue to own property in another state and thus could be subject to double taxation at death.

Example: Bob J. owns a home in New Hampshire but retires to Florida which he establishes as his principal domicile. He puts title to the old home (which he rents) in a revocable trust. When he dies, the trust, not Bob, will remain the owner. The trustee handles all details and Bob escapes double taxation.

Irrevocable Trust. This cannot be changed or revoked. The only control the donor has is the imposition of conditions on the use of the gift. These have to be carefully limited to avoid trouble with IRS. The property involved is considered a gift and so not subject to estate taxes. The beneficiary pays the taxes on distributed income.

Short-Term Trust. This is an irrevocable trust that runs for at least ten years or the lifetime of the beneficiary. The principal reverts to the grantor at termination. This can be valuable when you are contributing to the support of someone else, such as an elderly relative.

Example: Gene G. is contributing $250 per month to help his 75-year-old widowed mother. He is in the 50 percent tax bracket so has to make $6,000 a year for this gift—a 12 percent return on a $50,000 investment. Gene transfers $25,000 from his portfolio to a short-term trust with his mother as beneficiary. She gets the $3,000 annual income but pays no income tax. Gene now has an extra $25,000 working for his own benefit. When his mother dies—or after ten years if she is still living —the assets go back to Gene.

Clifford Trust. This is a variation of the short-term, reversionary trust. It is often used by affluent grandparents to help pay for the education of grandchildren and, not incidentally, to save taxes. With proper planning, the assets can be taken back at retirement (see table 14–5).

Example: At age 55, Charlie D. puts $10,000 in a Clifford Trust for his 7-year-old grandson. The money is invested in bonds to yield 12 percent. Each year, the child receives $1,200 and has no taxes to pay. If Charlie, who is in the 40 percent tax bracket, kept the money, his annual income tax on that return would be $480.

When he retires at age 65, Charlie gets back the $10,000 to enhance his income.

It is also possible to establish a trust with an outright gift. The assets become the property of the child, and the amount is considered, by IRS, as a gift of future income that those funds will earn. This is calculated at about 44 percent of the principal; in this case, $4,400: $10,000 × .44. As long as this figure is below $10,000 ($20,000 for a couple), there will be no gift tax.

Totten Trust. This is a bank account established by one person in trust for another, without formal agreement. It is a tentative trust that can

Table 14–5. **Tax Savings with a Clifford Trust**

	($10,000 investment, 10 years)			
Principal Invested at Yield of	Interest Income Accumulated After Taxes Parent's Tax Bracket			
	30%	40%	50%	Clifford Trust
8%	$ 7,244	$ 5,981	$4,802	$11,278
10	9,672	7,908	6,291	14,905
12	12,406	10,042	7,908	18,916

NOTE: Interest is compounded. Assumes that child has no other income. Tax savings apply only to parents.

SOURCE: Siegel & Mendlowitz, CPA, New York, N.Y.

be revoked anytime until the depositor dies or completes the gift. There's no cost, and in a savings account, the money can earn interest.

The trust can be set up for your spouse with yourself as trustee or by a parent for a child or grandchild . . . again with the donor as trustee. As creator of the trust, the donor has the right to dip into the account whenever he needs money.

When the donor dies, an adult beneficiary gets the money without problems. But when the beneficiary is a minor and the account involves less than $1,000, the money can be paid only to the minor's parent, parents or guardian. Above that amount, the parent or guardian must post bond and make a full report to the court.

Uniform Gifts to Minors. This is not exactly a trust but it accomplishes the same purpose for affluent folks. It is a gift to a minor child under the custody of an older relative or friend who has broad powers of investment. Ideally, there should be one gift, but it's permissable to make annual additions.

Again, the advantage is that the child will pay no taxes until the income is over $1,000 ($1,100 when there are dividends). Thereafter, the tax starts at a low 14 percent rate.

The child owns the property so that, at maturity, age 18 in most states, he or she has the sole responsibility for its disposition. Your daughter could take off for Europe with her unemployed boyfriend or your son could blow it all on a sports car. But such sad situations seldom occur. Most youngsters realize that this money is for their education.

With all types of trusts, consult your lawyer first and recognize that, usually, you lose control of both income and principal, but you can aid someone you love and may reduce your taxes.

Charitable Gifts

In working years, most people make charitable gifts as part of their personal philosophy, in discharge of their community responsibilities or in response to social or business pressures. A generous family might allocate 10 percent of gross income to church/synagogue, college, United Way, hospital or social agency. For an average family, the same percentage might be used against net income. Either way, the tax benefits can be important because gifts to IRS-qualified charities or institutions are tax deductible in the year they are made. Every donated dollar provides savings, as well as satisfaction.

After retirement, these contributions will probably have to be scaled back. But charitable giving can still be worthwhile. There are opportunities to make gifts that will provide income, as well as tax savings.

Pooled-income Plans (PIP). These are trusts set up by eleemosynary and educational institutions that provide life income for the donors with the principal going to the institution at the death of the donor/beneficiary. They can be worthwhile when you have ample assets and can get along on income somewhat less than the amount you could earn by your own investments.

As I pointed out in soliciting funds for my alma mater: The basic idea of GIVE WHILE YOU LIVE is to assure steady income for as long as you and/or your wife live, to set up tax benefits now and at death to leave something worthwhile to the university.

The university will invest the donation (or more likely, the receipts of its sale) in a professionally managed fund. The income, payable at periodic intervals, will be based on earnings, currently around 8 percent but *lower* if the investment performance declines; *higher,* if it improves. Thus, for every $10,000 gift, the annual yield will be about $800.

There are important tax benefits: (1) deduction of the current value of the gift on your income tax in the year of contribution; (2) lower estate administration costs since you'll leave less; (3) no capital gains tax on the higher-than-cost value when you give appreciated property.

The amount of the tax deduction is computed by IRS tables. It depends on age (yours and that of your spouse) and the highest rate of return made by the fund over the past three years. It will range from a high of about 59 percent ($5,900 for every $10,000) for a widower to a low of about 32 percent (when the wife is several years younger than the husband).

Charitable Trust. This is a separate, individual variation of PIP. It provides for a fixed percentage of assets as income to the donor and ownership of the assets by the institution. The income is variable because the market value of the property may fluctuate. The percentage return cannot be changed after the trust is established. The higher the percentage of payout, the greater the annual income but the smaller the charitable deduction.

Charitable Remainder Annuity Trust. This is similar to the charitable trust but the income is a fixed sum, paid at least annually, rather than a percentage of assets. Each payment is treated as a partial return of principal and thus tax exempt with the balance taxable income.

Louis Baruch Rubinstein, the lawyer who reviewed this chapter, notes, "It is important to adher strictly to IRS requirements which are both mandatory and optional. The annual fixed payments must be at least 5 percent of the value of the trust assets, either from present or accumulated income. If income is insufficient, these are taken from the principal. They must be paid to one or more specified beneficiaries, at least one of which is not a charity."

Give While You Live

At this point, let me inject a bit of personal philosophy that applies to most, but not all, retirees: when you give while you live, you combine the joy of aiding someone or some institution/cause with tax savings. Many retirees have more assets than they need and their children are making more money than they ever did. With proper planning, these retirees are in a position to pass on a worthwhile inheritance and still make substantial charitable gifts.

The timing of gifts depends on your resources and the ages of both partners. If your liquid assets—those that do, or can, provide income (securities, real estate, paid-up life insurance, etc.)—are close to the $450,000 in the "On Easy Street" column in table 14–3, you can start soon after quitting work. If these assets total about $275,000 ("All is Well" column), better wait until age 75. Always be realistic—not too optimistic or too pessimistic—about how long you will live. Much as we like to look forward to many more years, we must recognize that only half of us will beat the averages: at age 75, a life expectancy of 8.6 years for men; 11.5 for women.

Making Your Own Calculations

If you are still hesitant about depleting assets:

1. Calculate the income you can count on: Social Security, pension and return on investments; say, $12,000, $6,000 and $12,000, respectively, which is a total of $30,000 a year. The Social Security and pension benefits will be less after the death of the primary wage earner but so will expenses.

2. Project your annual expenses at a 5 percent inflation rate. If you can live comfortably on $20,000, you will need $25,600 in five years; $32,600 in ten years. THESE ARE MAXIMUMS.

In the example, substantial gifts would be a bit risky when the husband is under 75. If gifts are made, the income will be less: $1,200 a year for each $10,000 gift (assuming that 12 percent yield).

3. With your tax adviser, find out how much you can afford to give under a PIP. Roughly, this will cut your income by one-third: an 8 percent return versus a 12 percent yield if you stand pat.

4. Determine how long your capital will last if you invade principal. With a 12 percent yield, you can withdraw 15 percent a year of your invested assets for almost fourteen years before there will be nothing left. That means you can afford to give away at least $3,000 annually.

5. If you prefer to start with what you want to leave to your children, calculate your total assets and then specify, in your will, what you want to go to the children and bequeath the balance to charity.

I realize that such generosity does not anticipate heavy medical expenses, but the odds are eleven to one that such costs will NOT occur. It's O.K. to be conservative but not overly so. You can't take it with you.

These calculations become more meaningful after the death of the first spouse. The survivor's income may be less, but after the first death, there is need to protect only one person.

Making substantial gifts is difficult at any age. Most people spend their lives trying to accumulate wealth and, psychologically, find it hard to alter their philosophy. But remember that, at the death of the surviving partner, cherished possessions will probably be sold for a fraction of their value by an unknown professional. Judging from what I've seen in retirement communities, too many people die with too much wealth. They can afford to give while they live.

When You Move to Another State

When people retire in the same state where they have been living, estate planning should not be too difficult. You and your spouse know where most documents/property are located; your lawyer should be familiar with your resources and wishes; your survivor will be known at the bank and trust company; and your heirs can ask for help from old friends.

But when you move to a new state, it is essential to start at A and touch all the bases to take advantage of tax breaks and to avoid future problems such as double taxation. When you establish a new principal domicile:

In the old state:

- Sell or transfer title of property to your children or a trust.
- Close out bank and savings accounts.

- Change addresses for all securities, real estate, pensions, etc.
- Notify the state departments responsible for car registration, drivers' licenses and income tax returns.

In the new state:

- Apply for a certificate of domicile at the county clerk's office. This is imperative when there's a homestead exemption for residents over age 65.
- Change the registration of your car and drivers' licenses.
- Open a savings and checking account in the new community.
- Transfer securities to a safe deposit box in that new bank. But do not include foreign stocks or bonds because, if you die, the estate cannot transfer them without clearance from foreign authorities.
- Register to vote and, later, vote.
- File estimated federal income tax returns from your new address.
- Arrange for Social Security and pension checks to be sent to your new address or to the new bank.
- Retain a local lawyer to review your will and other legal documents and to advise you on special local situations such as homestead exemptions and over-65 benefits.

One Final Comment

An estate plan is a separate entity, related to, but not a substitute for, a financial plan. While you live, you can control most of your expenses and investments, but after you are gone, the law, and lawyers, take over. If you really love your family, one of the most meaningful actions to take is to prepare, affirm and maintain an estate plan for yourself, your spouse and your children. What you do NOW will determine what they can, or cannot, do in the future.

15. Your Safe Deposit Box—
and Power of Attorney

A safe deposit box is a *must* for everyone. In today's complex world with ever-changing legal and governmental requirements and family mobility, an increasing number of documents and records are needed to assure benefits and avoid penalties. Deeds, receipts and policies must be readily available. A safe deposit box not only provides protection for valuables but can be useful in organizing your financial affairs. As we grow older, we tend to mislay or misfile important papers. By placing these in appropriately marked envelopes in a safe deposit box, you can save yourself future frustration and your heirs and executor time and money. Ideally, your lock box should contain almost everything you would hate to lose (assuming it's small enough to fit) and nothing that you or your survivors wish wasn't there.

At death, a safe deposit box can be opened by the spouse, executor or known heir only in the presence of a bank officer and for the specific purpose of locating essential documents. The banker must sign a receipt for removed articles and make this available to tax authorities. The box is then sealed and reopened under the surveillance of a government official, usually from the tax office. If he sees piles of cash or jewelry and your spouse or other authorized person cannot prove ownership, there can be real trouble.

To protect your family and double-check yourself, arrange for regular access to the lock box by a trustworthy individual who is in a position to know the contents: spouse, son, daughter, attorney or executor.

Always review every item before it's stored and after there's been a major change in your family life: a new job, a new home, retirement, divorce, a new member of the family—by birth or marriage—and so forth. If you have any doubts as to the future need of any item, check with your attorney. You want to save what's useful, but you don't want to start a collection.

DO Deposit:

• Permanent personal documents: certificates of birth, citizenship and marriage. You'll need these to fill out claims and collect benefits.

• Military discharge and service records: for veterans benefits and for burial in a national cemetery.

• Title papers involving purchase, ownership and sale of real estate, automobiles, valuable collections, etc.

• Securities or proof of ownership of shares of corporations held by your broker or by investment companies.

• Loan agreements such as mortgages, installment sales contracts, or personal loans to others.

• Certificates stating the value of jewelry, fur coats and other expensive items that will become part of your estate.

• Legal papers.

• Jewelry not worn frequently.

DO NOT Put in:

• Your original will. A copy is O.K. but the original should be readily available at death: in a home file or, better, in your lawyer's office.

• Tax returns of recent years. It's bothersome when you have to refer to these in a hurry.

• Outdated wills or agreements that have been superseded by other legal documents—destroy them.

• Deed to the cemetery plot.

If you store jewelry or negotiable securities, make sure that the bank carries insurance. If not, ask your insurance agent to add a rider to your homeowner's policy. The cost is about $50 per $100,000.

Power of Attorney

No estate plan is complete without granting someone power of attorney to act in your behalf if you are unable or unwilling to do so through absence, illness or inconvenience. Preferably, the agent should be an individual, but it can be an institution.

The actions taken by this agent are binding on you, but the power can be revoked at any time and is automatically voided when you die or lose your mental facilities. Before retirement, a power of attorney is useful; after retirement, it is essential.

The delegation of power is easy and follows a simple legal form whereby you appoint someone to be "true, sufficient and lawful attor-

ney . . . to borrow in my name, to buy and sell securities or property
. . . to sign checks . . . to conduct banking affairs . . . to discharge claims
. . . to enter into contracts, etc." This standard language can be amended
to meet specific needs.

Usually, the power of attorney is given to a relative or, in business,
to a partner. If the relative lives far away, you may want to arrange for
more than one person to be designated, but this can create problems.
The individual should not only be honest and loyal but should be familiar with the areas where he/she has power to act. For personal affairs,
this could be a husband or wife, son or daughter; for investments, a
lawyer, broker or investment adviser.

But when you name someone outside your family, be slow and
skeptical. A stockbroker depends on commissions for his income, so
there's a temptation to buy and sell frequently. Investors are protected
against churning (too-frequent transactions), but in erratic stock markets, this can be hard to prove . . . and costly.

Make such a decision only after careful evaluation of the experience,
record and philosophy of the individual or organization. Then, follow
all transactions for six months and if you are not satisfied, end the
arrangement. And when you do revoke the document, do so in writing
with copies to all those with whom the agent had dealings.

The power of attorney is especially valuable when: (1) you go on an
extended trip and will not be kept aware of developments; (2) property
is jointly owned because, by law, when one person is incapacitated, the
other cannot act alone; (3) you are single with no relatives or when your
family is far away. In retirement areas, financial institutions often accept this responsibility directly or as trustee for savings/investments
. . . for ample fees.

Caveats

• Always consult a lawyer before naming as attorney someone who
is already a trustee or beneficiary of a trust you established. His/her role
could be challenged, by other relatives, as a conflict of interest.

• Do not name your spouse unless your marriage is sound. If there's
a break-up, the assets may be spent before you can revoke the assign-
ment.

• If you have any qualms about the integrity or ability of the agent,
have the lawyer add a protection clause: that you will back and make
good only those transactions specifically authorized.

• If you prefer to have the power of attorney take effect only when you become incapacitated, be sure that nothing is done until some responsible authority has declared you incapable of managing your own affairs.

A power of attorney can be a valuable tool in estate planning but do not assign it or accept it unless you understand the full commitment: that the attorney always has the right to act in your behalf.

V.

—

WHERE TO LIVE

For most people, their home is their largest asset, their most rewarding investment, their best tax shelter, an excellent hedge against inflation, and an important factor in a sense of family security. But not everyone can afford, or will prefer, to own a home.

The benefits of home ownership are recognized because: (1) surveys show that, in many areas, 80 percent of families headed by a male, aged 65, own their homes and 90 percent of these have paid off the mortgage; (2) the appreciation in the value of their homes is the main reason why so many retirees can look forward to a financially secure retirement; (3) generally, the prices of houses have increased faster than the rate of inflation.

There's no guarantee that such benefits will continue, but as long as housing remains in short supply, ownership should pay off. There are, of course, negatives: (1) all real estate is an illiquid investment that is easy to get into but hard to get out of; (2) homes themselves do not provide income that often is essential in retirement; (3) older properties with rising costs of maintenance and repairs, can drain limited resources.

Before retirement owning a home can be the keystone of successful financial planning. *After retirement,* this may not always be the wisest use of assets.

The best time to start discussion of the future of your home is at age 60. Before then, most people have difficulty in accepting the harsh facts of retirement: that the day will come when they will no longer be physically able to move easily or do as much; that financial resources will be spent more for needs than wants; and that there will be a steady loss of old friends.

This does not mean that you should panic or become despondent. If you are a worrier, you will be upset anyway. But the cold statistics are that, starting at about age 70, the average retiree will feel poorly five weeks a year and in two of those weeks will need help from someone else. Basically, the first decision should be whether to stay in the old homestead or to move elsewhere.

16. Stay or Move?

By the time you pass age 60, you probably live where you want in the type of home you prefer. Since home is where the heart is, any move will be difficult.

There will be valid financial reasons for staying: you know your expenses and feel that you can keep them under control; the mortgage is, or soon will be, paid off; there will be no major expenses for moving, new furniture, rugs, draperies, etc.

If you are renting, the situation is similar but more tenuous because you cannot feel as secure, will face ever-higher costs and if the building is sold, may have to buy should the apartment be turned into a condominium.

Dollarwise, it will probably pay you to sell your home at a hefty profit. If you are over age 55 and have lived in the house three of the last five years, there will be no income tax to pay on the first $125,000 of the capital gain. If you are younger and buy a more expensive home, the tax can be postponed . . . as will be outlined later.

With the proceeds of the sale, you can fulfill lifelong dreams such as a luxurious vacation. Or, if you're more practical, you can use part of the money to make a down payment on a new home. In both cases, you should be able to have extra funds for investments to provide added income.

It's true that, if you stay, your property will probably continue to increase in value, but to make it worthwhile that average annual rate of gain should be greater than can be obtained from investing: currently, a minimum of 11 percent a year. This is the net return available from tax-free municipal bonds and, for many retirees, the after-tax yield of fixed income investments such as Treasury bills, bonds and some certificates of deposit.

In making these comparisons, deduct the broker's commission on the sale of your old home (usually about 7 percent) and some closing costs on the new one.

Example: You bought your house for $35,000. It's now worth $108,000. After commissions and fees, a sale would net about $100,000. If the mortgage is paid off, that money could bring in an annual after-tax income of $10,000 to $12,000.

A mortgage-free home is mentally satisfying but financially costly. You cannot spend that unrealized appreciation. Unless and until the house is sold, the only people who will benefit will be your heirs!

A sale is, usually, logical, but, with few exceptions, the decision to stay or move will be based on personal factors: *on the positive side,* comfort, convenience, safety and security; *on the negative,* fear, neighborhood deterioration, higher taxes, loneliness and inability to cope.

If you stay, you will be in familiar territory; your family will probably be close by; you will have friends at your church/synagogue and club, respect in your community and, generally, will feel comfortable and secure.

But how long will such pleasure continue? Neighborhoods deteriorate, taxes soar, loneliness increases as old friends die or move and, most devastating, you may no longer be as important as you were.

This isolation is especially galling to executives, as explained by Edward Streeter in his entertaining book, *Chairman of the Board:*

> The duties and obligations that we complained of so bitterly suddenly appear in a new light now that we are about to be relieved of them. The great dinners at the Waldorf, the relaxed atmosphere of "21", the ball games in the company's box . . . the flying business trips around the country, the request for favors that somehow must be granted . . . now appear nostalgically in the soft amber of our setting sun. . . . The men with whom we sat through the years on commercial and charitable boards and club committees . . . will no longer occupy an established place in the community . . . unwanted and unneeded, not because people don't like us but because their financial attachment was to Crombie, Hamilton and Gardner, the institution rather than to Graham Crombie, the man.

It's easy to say that every individual and family should choose logically but it seldom works out that way. Too often, major decisions are delayed until action is forced by circumstances. That is not wise financial planning.

Checklists for Staying or Moving

To provide some guidelines for discussion of both the old and new location, here are factors that are important to comfortable retirement in any location. Use them first in rating your present home and, later, to judge the alternatives (with appropriate revisions). They should be studied together with the checklists on what you want to do in retirement.

Table 16–1.   Checklist for Community or Area

Community	Good	Fair	Poor
Clean, well-managed municipality	———	———	———
Friendly people	———	———	———
Good MDs, DDs, hospitals	———	———	———
Recreational facilities			
Golf	———	———	———
Tennis	———	———	———
Swimming	———	———	———
Bowling	———	———	———
Sailing	———	———	———
Fishing	———	———	———
Other	———	———	———
Cultural opportunities			
Library	———	———	———
Theater	———	———	———
Art	———	———	———
Education	———	———	———
Music	———	———	———
Other	———	———	———
Area/section			
Weather	———	———	———
Clean/well-managed	———	———	———
Proud to live here?	———	———	———
Does something for me?	———	———	———
Neighbors with common interest	———	———	———
Church/synagogue	———	———	———
Convenient shopping	———	———	———
Accessible transportation			
Buses	———	———	———
Highways	———	———	———
Airport	———	———	———
Pets welcome?			

In your present location, before writing any answer, review the questions and then walk around the neighborhood, recall how it looked five years ago and how it is likely to be in another decade.

Later, when you have zeroed in on possible new sites, be just as methodical and candid. Ideally, a retirement move should be for life, but realistically, it may be a shorter period.

Your answers should reflect your needs, wants and prejudices. The new young families in the old neighborhood may be converting eyesores into attractive homes, but if they oust old friends and familiar stores and bring in scores of children, such changes will not be welcome.

Checklist for Home After Retirement

Neighborhood

    In the past five years, has the area: Improved

                                              Remained stable

                                              Deteriorated

    How do you anticipate it will be in ten years: Better

                                              About same

                                            Worse

    If your answer is better, why?

        Urban redevelopment

        Renovation (such as restoration of brownstones in Brooklyn)

        Other

    If your answer is worse, why?

        Influx of young families with noisy children?

        Intrusion of commercial/apartment buildings?

        Other

Stores/services

    Are they expanding?   improving?   declining?

    In ten years, will they be satisfactory?

Municipal Services

    In the past five years, have they: Improved

                                         Stayed about same

                                         Deteriorated

Transportation

    In the past five years, has the situation: Improved

                                         Stayed about same

                                         Deteriorated

Medical/hospital services: Convenient

                       Difficult to reach

Home: General

    Is the house too large?   a maximum of three bedrooms and, preferably, two, unless you have a large family

    Are there too many stairs to climb?   a maximum of five steps to the second floor or basement

Checklist—*Continued*

Is there a bath and bedroom on the first floor?

Are there too many windows?   to clean and to cover with storm
windows

Is the house difficult and expensive to maintain?   in need of
frequent repairs?   large lawn to mow
and garden to tend?

Do the bathroom and kitchen need remodeling?

Are the plumbing and electrical systems in good shape?

Will the roof have to be replaced?

Are the furnace and air conditioners adequate and good for ten
years?

Home: Specific

Windows: low enough to see out to a garden or lawn but not so low as
to welcome intruders: double-glazed and insulated to save on
heating and cooling; with wide, water-impervious sills for
safety and to accommodate planters and flower pots

Electrical outlets: 18 inches from the floor to eliminate the necessity of
stooping

Lighting: three times as much as designed for younger families

Doorknobs: big, lever-type, hexagonal or octagonal for easy gripping

Doors: wide enough to accommodate a wheelchair

Floors: nonskid unglazed ceramic or unwaxed vinyl tile and firmly an-
chored rugs and carpets

Kitchen: with labor/step-saving items such as a self-cleaning range with
easy-to-reach controls; single mixing faucet; handy cabinets
and shelves; a dining corner or breakfast bar

Bathrooms: safe, step-in tub with grab bars in the wall; nonslip stripping
on the bottom of the tub and shower; shower with seat; sizeable, easy-to-open medicine chest: light switch outside the door
and a nightlight between the bedroom and bathroom

Bedrooms: preferably two to allow privacy and permit sick care; close to
bathroom; good light from windows or lamps for reading;
space enough for two dressers; a small cabinet and plenty of
storage space with sliding closet doors

Workroom: good ventilation and heating; overhead light; at least three
electrical outlets well above the floor

Checklist—*Continued*

> Garage: near the street with automatic door and rain-protected
> passage into the house
> Patio: private enough to permit sunbathing; built-in fireplace or
> barbecue pit
> Safety features: smoke detector, fire alarm and automatic dialing
> system on the telephone to summon help if needed

And that new community may be exciting and attractive now, but how will it be when you are no longer able to drive a car?

Moving

With a new home, there are two broad choices: to move nearby to a condominium, smaller home or apartment where you can retain friendships and community involvement or pull up stakes and head to a new area.

For those who have deep roots or prefer the security of familiarity, the first step is probably wise. Presumably, the new home will be smaller, less expensive, more convenient and better adapted to after-work living. The move should be *to* something better, not *away* from an unsatisfactory situation. Moving is difficult, expensive and upsetting. It should not be done on a temporary basis unless there are strong reasons for compromise, such as the reluctance of one partner.

Historically, only about 15 percent of retirees move, but this is changing rapidly as more people look for the warm weather and easy living of the South, Southwest and Far West. And the financial factors of the new location are usually favorable: cheaper housing, fewer material needs and more available, less expensive recreation. But many of these savings are the result of changes in lifestyle rather than lower costs.

In most cases, you can effect the same economies if you stay in your old home and live at a more leisurely, more informal, less competitive pace. This is hard to do because of habit, the feeling that you must keep up with your still-working neighbors and the tendency to do things that you were unable to enjoy before retirement.

As explained by one of my Yale classmates who lives in a northern New Jersey suburb: "Since I quit work, our expenses for entertainment have nearly doubled. We go to the opera, see Broadway plays, dine at good restaurants and attend almost every golf tournament and dance at the country club—all things we never had time for earlier. They are expensive, require a new wardrobe every few months and involve considerable entertaining as we make it a point to look up old friends to join us. With ever-higher costs and a more or less fixed income, we may not be able to continue this merry pace. We may have to move to change our lifestyle."

When you choose a new community, you can dictate your own lifestyle. This applies especially to retirement areas where there are few pressures to compete and to attain status other than by personal involvement that does not require substantial expenditures. You can scale your lifestyle according to your income/wishes. If money is tight, you can catch fish or raise vegetables. For recreation, you can go to a public beach, play golf on a low-fee public course or just relax in the sun. When you entertain, you can serve wine and cheese or broil hamburgers over an outdoor grill. Such a simple lifestyle may require some adjustments (especially for the socially conscious), but it will be accepted and acceptable. And since most of your neighbors are in similar circumstances, you can join them at community picnics and pancake breakfasts costing $1.50 each.

Of course, if you can afford it, you can choose an area where there are private clubs and frequent social functions.

New Location

There are extra costs in relocation: for the actual moving, $3,000 to $5,000; for the purchase of a house or condominium or security deposits on an apartment; for new furniture and furnishings (if needed or wanted), and so on. All of these factors should be considered before retirement when there will be a regular paycheck to buy modern appliances and to set up a special, savings-for-the-new-home account.

Even when you plan to stay put, you should take a look at possible new locations when you are in your early 60s. Most people tend to start their search in communities where they have friends. This exploration should take place only when you have a fairly clear idea of what you want and how much you can afford as determined by the checklists.

When you visit potential areas, do so on vacation when you are likely to be as relaxed and recreation-minded as you hope to be in retirement. If you both like warm weather, drive to Florida and then work along the Gulf coast. Next year, start in the Southwest and end in Southern California.

If you prefer changing seasons, drive from Maine to the Carolinas or in reverse. In year 2, wander around the Middle West and in year 3, motor along the northern Pacific Coast.

This sounds like a lot of traveling but since you can expect to live another fifteen to twenty years, it is worthwhile.

Whether you buy or rent, you will have to pay extra if:

- *You want an address:* Carmel, Monterey or La Jolla in California; Delray Beach or Stuart in Florida; St. Simon's or Hilton Head in the Carolinas, etc.
- *You want a view:* of mountains, sea, golf course or lake. If this is what you dreamed of, the few extra dollars will not be *that* important. In effect, you are swapping $100 per $1,000 savings, and a smaller estate for your heirs, for what, hopefully, will be years of extra pleasure.
- *You opt for convenience:* within walking distance of a pool, golf course, community center, stores, library, and so on. You will save on transportation costs, but there may be more traffic, more people and more noise.

Think ahead: how will this site, these services be in ten years when you may not be able to fully enjoy all of these extras or will welcome them even more? Will you be able to afford them?

Specific Community

Once you have zeroed in on two or three communities, find out all you can about its services, organizations, type of residents, lifestyle and probable future. Generally, the character of an area is slow to change. If the lawns are neat and the houses painted, the chances are that such pride will continue. But if there are one or two large dwellings with unkempt trees and banging shutters, be careful. These could be the first sign of neighborhood deterioration. To double-check, find a way to look at several backyards. When there are trash piles, topless garbage cans and abandoned furniture, the owners are not likely to be concerned about future property values. And if there are oil drips on the driveways, you'll have to get used to unsightly cars being repaired over weekends.

These caveats seem obvious, but it is surprising how often they are subordinated to price, prestige or pressure . . . from your family or the real estate agent. They are especially important with a retirement home because, in most cases, this is where you will spend the rest of your life.

Check out areas carefully and more than once. Make at least two visits: spend two weeks there in winter and a week in the summer. Tourists can clog highways and stores in February, but in July some communities can be deserted and lonesome. Drive around, walk around, talk to the storekeepers and chat with folks, old and young. Visit the local library to see what types of books they have. Wander down side streets and see how people keep their grounds, whether they have lovely gardens and if they use shrubs to block off their neighbors. These explorations will be valuable in learning about traffic, the variety of community services, the scope and skill of municipal services: how often do you see a policeman or squad car? how many potholes are in the street? is garbage uncollected in the late afternoon?

Pay heed to religious and educational centers. If you are a Unitarian, you won't be happy in a town dominated by fundamentalist preachers. If you hope to brush up on your Greek, make sure that the community college has such courses.

Contact the chamber of commerce and get a list of major businesses and projected developments to learn if they are the type that might make part-time use of your skills and experience, if a new highway may come close to the back of your potential property or that lovely lake front will soon be lined with condominiums. Keep that ten-year future in focus.

When you go back home, subscribe to the local newspaper to learn about taxes, local political issues and what residents feel about planning. Hopefully, you are going to live there for a long time.

New Home or Old Home Area

New housing developments are always more attractive because the buildings and facilities are bright and exciting. But do not neglect older areas as long as they are stable and well maintained. They will be more convenient to services and recreational facilities and, generally, less expensive. You will be acquiring an older house with used appliances, but there will probably be an established garden with trees and shrubs that will not require much care.

Retirement Communities

So far, we've centered on more or less standard living areas, but you may prefer a retirement community where all residents are adults and you won't be bothered with children, noise and disruption . . . all of increasing annoyance as you grow older.

The condominiums/houses/apartments will be look-alikes, but common areas will be landscaped and well kept and, usually, there will be special recreational, educational and cultural programs.

To enjoy living in these enclaves, you must be somewhat of a conformist and be ready to accept the mores, platitudes, prejudices and routines of the establishment. In the early years of retirement, some of these communal pressures will not be welcome. You may want to relax, make your own friends, set your own pace and retain your own privacy. But as you grow older and learn to accept your neighbors (loving some and enduring others), you will appreciate the prepared schedules and organized events. For a widow or widower, these can be welcome and enjoyable. There will always be some friend who cares.

Look for these extra features:

Club/community center. This brings people together, makes it possible to find and keep friends and to be involved with others, in card games, discussion groups, craft classes and sports.

Be sure that the building/pool/putting green are in operation or under construction. And get full details of membership and maintenance. Are the annual dues part of the cost of your home? Do you and your neighbors control operations and the budget? If not, that original annual levy of $300 may jump to $1,000!

Maintenance. No worries about lawn and ground care. At 65, you will probably prefer to handle these chores yourself, but at 75, it may be neither easy nor possible. Here again, find out how costs are negotiated, allocated and controlled.

In most new retirement communities, these special services are handled through a community association. In the early years, this will be controlled by the developer with token representation by homeowners. Have your lawyer check the agreement, and if you move there, mark the date when the annual meeting is held and get organized to take control as early as you and your neighbors can.

Endowment Care

A special type of retirement community is one that offers complete living/health services on payment of an endowment plus a monthly fee. Usually, these are high-rise buildings with recreational, therapeutic, health and dining services. You are sure of room, board and round-the-clock medical/nursing care as long as you and your spouse live.

Everything is designed for senior citizens: sloping ramps, wide elevators, grab rails in the bath and high railings on the porches. Each unit has its own kitchen for breakfast and snacks, and you get one meal a day in the common dining room.

Soon after you reach age 60, make it a point to visit one of these projects. You will not be ready for such care but it's one of the best ways I know to understand the problems of age and why it is so important to plan where you will live after work. You and your spouse may shudder at the thought of confinement to a wheelchair, but it's a possibility that should be considered long before it happens.

Costs depend on the size of the dwelling unit and number of occupants. Typically, a two-room efficiency requires a cash outlay of about $35,000 with a monthly fee of $400 for a single person plus $170 per month more for the second occupant. Deluxe, two bedroom, two bath suites start at $70,000 with monthly fees of around $600 for a couple.

For an extra payment, you can arrange for a death reimbursement option: if you die within four years of occupancy, the endowment will be repaid on a prorata basis.

These controlled, everything's-available communities are worthwhile for those who are ill or fear disability or who want a sense of security. But once you move there, you will have a difficult time getting out.

Types of Dwellings

These descriptions are keyed to retirement living, but they also apply to homes while you are working.

House. A house is yours to do with what you will. It's also a responsibility and must be maintained, inside and out. That's fine if you are handy with tools, but it can be expensive and irritating if you have to hire a carpenter, plumber or gardener. Always look at your choice in terms of total costs and total involvement and, again, that ten-year time frame.

Condominium. This will be convenient, relatively inexpensive and easy to maintain. But you are buying group living. You must conform to certain rules and accept your share of joint expenses: for exterior upkeep, parking, roof, furnace/air conditioner, and so on.

Before you buy, get a written explanation of all communal costs, reserve funds for replacements and schedules of assessments. If sufficient money has not been set aside for new equipment and repairs, you may have to come up with $1,500 or more for a new roof or air-conditioner. A condo may be like a home, but it's part of a joint enterprise and you have only one vote.

Apartment. This can be ideal if you: (1) plan to split your time between the retirement area and your old home or vacation cottage; (2) can slim down furniture, furnishings and possessions to fit a smaller space—a difficult task for some people who insist on retaining mementos, files and heirlooms, but storage can be expensive and, often, damaging; (3) expect to be away frequently on trips or visits and want the security and availability of neighbors and a superintendent; (4) do not want to be bothered with repairs and maintenance.

With an apartment, the checklist is not as important as with a home or condominium because it's usually easy to move. But always look for good services such as trash collection, regular painting and security.

It's also wise to meet your neighbors before you sign a lease. You may find yourself next to a night owl who keeps his radio and TV on full blast.

And, if you can do so, try to arrange some protection against exorbitant rent increases by means of written escalation clauses for the next three to five years.

Mobile Home. In the right location, these can be pleasant places to live. At the outset, you may be a bit hesitant, but if you take time to visit some of these communities and look inside these homes, you will be surprised at their comfort, convenience and low costs—to buy and to maintain.

On the average, a mobile home suitable for a retired couple, will cost under $50,000, including land and installation. The quality of these units is improving. The Department of Housing and Urban Development (HUD) has construction standards to make them safer and more durable and, to meet consumer requests, the buildings are wider, windows larger and designs more livable.

Most important, financing of mobile homes, especially in retirement areas, is easy and inexpensive with mortgages as long as thirty years with as little as 5 percent down. By making a large down payment with the cash from the sale of your old home, you can arrange a mortgage where total payments—for interest, amortization, insurance and taxes—can be as low as $150 per month. In most cases, this will be less than you've been paying.

By checking ads and visiting around, you can find a project that will include recreational facilities: a swimming pool, tennis and shuffleboard courts and, for a low membership fee, a golf course.

And if you want to keep heirlooms and extra clothing, you can rent an individual locker room at a nearby storage area.

17. Rent or Buy?

The choice of renting or buying a home depends on your income and lifestyle. Ownership provides a sense of security, relatively fixed costs in that mortgage payments will stay about the same and increases will be primarily for taxes, repairs/upkeep/improvements, tax benefits from deductions for interest and real estate taxes and, most important, appreciation which will enrich your heirs more than yourselves.

But there are people who are unwilling or unable to make the necessary financial commitments or accept the responsibilities of ownership. They may pay less, but they face ever-higher costs which can be partially or fully offset by the extra income from the investment of the money that would be needed for a down payment on a purchase.

Here's how to compare costs of renting or buying: a $60,000 house or condominium purchased with $30,000 down (from the sale of the old house) plus $30,000 from a fifteen-year mortgage at 16 percent.

Annual Cost of Ownership

Costs	Years 1–5	Years 6–10	Years 11–15
Mortgage payments	$5,289	$5,289	$5,289
Insurance	150	150	150
Maintenance/repairs	1,000	1,200	1,500
Real estate taxes	1,000	1,200	1,500
Total	7,439	7,839	8,439
Deductible:			
Interest (average)	4,545	3,650	1,662
Real estate taxes	1,000	1,200	1,500
Total deductible	5,545	4,850	3,162
Net cost	$1,894	$2,989	$5,277

SOURCE: Based on data from U.S. Department of Labor.

Note how the net cost rises as the deductions for interest decline. Hopefully, of course, this will be offset by an increase in the value of the property, but you can't spend this money!

Renting is much more expensive at the outset but the difference narrows over the years. Let's say, an apartment/condominium can be rented at increasing rates: for the first five years, $700 per month; $800 for the next five years and $900 for the eleventh through fifteenth years. Annually, these figures are $8,400, $9,600 and $10,800. These costs are reduced by the interest earned on the investment of the $30,000 down payment: $3,600 a year (at 12 percent), so the net costs are $4,800, $6,000 and $7,200 a year . . . all more than the costs of ownership. But the renter always has readily available funds for emergencies and does not have to worry about repairs, maintenance, and, at some point, the sale of property.

Dollarwise, ownership is best for retirees with high incomes: broadly, over $25,000 a year: $10,000 in Social Security (nontaxable); $5,000 in pension (partly taxable); and $10,000 from investments/personal pension (largely taxable). It is feasible for those with lower incomes when the returns on investments—dividends and interest—are taxable. But it is not worthwhile for those whose incomes are lower or tax exempt.

Owning a House While You Work

Now, let's step back a bit to see how home ownership, during working years, can be an important factor in successful financial planning. In fact, for most people, owning their home is their most rewarding investment. It combines a tax shelter with appreciation:

1. The purchase can be highly leveraged: a small down payment of 10 percent or so with the balance of the purchase price covered by a mortgage that is repaid with ever-depreciating dollars.

2. There are tax deductions, on federal, state, and local income tax returns, of two of the biggest expenses: interest and real estate taxes.

3. When the house is sold, the capital gains tax can be deferred and, eventually, eliminated.

Example: At age 35, Steve H., who works for a company where he can look forward to steady advancement and higher income, buys an $80,000 house with $10,000 down and a twenty-five-year mortgage at 12 percent.

His payments, to the lending institution, are $7,371 a year, or $641.25 per month. In the first year, most of this is tax-deductible interest. At a tax rate of 32 percent, this means annual benefits of some $2,359, so the monthly cost, in after-tax dollars, is $417.67. This does not count further deductions for real estate taxes. On his $10,000 cash investment, Steve will, in effect, get his money back in less than five years.

More important, Steve owns an ever-more-valuable asset. Every 10 percent rise in its price means a 80 percent annual rate of return on his own money: $8,000 on the $10,000 down payment. With good property, equity—the money value in excess of claims or liens against it—continues to grow steadily. In about nine years, Steve's equity will be greater than his purchase price.

These are maximum figures because the percentage of payments credited to interest drops steadily. By the end of the fifth year, interest will represent only 91 percent of the total; in ten years, 84 percent, etc.

The effect of this tax benefit is to lower the mortgage interest rate to an average of a little over 9 percent—just about the rate of inflation in recent years. In other words, a mortgaged home is a good way to beat or, at least, keep pace with, inflation.

Pyramiding Assets to Build a Retirement Fund

Now let's see how home ownership can help finance retirement. Let's assume that Steve bought in a booming area and that the value of his home rises 10 percent annually, to about $100,000 in five years. He sells his house and, after paying off the mortgage and the broker's fee, he nets $72,000. He uses $45,000 as a down payment on a new $175,000 home, takes out a $130,000 mortgage (for which he is eligible because of his higher salary) and invests the $27,000 in a deferred annuity to be paid out after retirement. He must file a capital gains tax report, but he will not have to pay a tax because the proceeds of the sale are less than the cost of his new home.

If Steve stays in the second house or repeats the process, he will be wise to delay the final sale until he is over 55 years old. At this age, he gets an additional tax break: no capital gains tax on the first $125,000 profit.

There is one possible flaw in this success story: that the value of the property(ies) will not rise. But unless there is an awesome depression, Steve should be able to sell his home, at or near retirement, for his $175,000 cost. By then, the mortgage will be paid off and he will have plenty of money to buy a smaller, less expensive retirement home: for cash if he and his wife prefer security; with a substantial down payment, say $50,000, and a fifteen-year mortgage if he wants to make better use of his resources. Even after buying new furniture, appliances, car, etc., Steve should have $100,000 to invest. At a 12 percent annual yield, that's $12,000 a year income: possibly less if he opts for tax-exempt bonds; more if he or his surviving spouse invade capital.

But if Steve sells before age 55, he will have to pay a tax on the capital gains unless he buys a more expensive house. Or if Mrs. H. should die when Steve is 54 and, at age 56, Steve marries a 55-year-old widow and both sell their homes to buy one new one, only one spouse can make use of the exclusion. Solution: one spouse should sell before the marriage.

Before you complete any major real estate sale, check with your tax adviser as there may be important costs or savings.

The right kind of home, bought at the right price with the right mortgage, can be an effective hedge against inflation, and one of the best tools of financial planning for retirement.

But the wrong kind of house in the wrong location can be dangerous and costly. Its value will decline, the pleasure of ownership can be destroyed if the neighborhood deteriorates and while there will still be money after its sale, the proceeds may not be enough to assure that financially secure retirement.

With all real estate, always project how the property and area will look in fifteen or twenty years hence and review your forecast every year. One of the great mistakes of older people is their refusal to sell their old home before its value declines.

How Much to Pay for Your Home

When you are close to retirement, start your calculations of housing with total annual costs. Keep these below 25 percent of your fixed income: i.e., under $5,000 ($417 per month) when you expect to receive $20,000 from Social Security, pension and investments. If you go much above this percentage, you will have to stint on some items, such as recreation and travel. And if you are a real conservative, set that 25 percent against the income the surviving spouse will have or buy life insurance that will pay off the mortgage when you die.

When you make your projections, factor in the future upkeep at an annual increase of 10 percent for the next three years. If you and/or your spouse are not willing, or able, to spend time on cleaning, painting, repairs and lawn and garden care, make that a 15 percent annual rise.

Generally, a new house will cost less to maintain and will appreciate faster than an older one. But if you are handy with tools, take a look at older homes in stable neighborhoods. They will probably be larger, better landscaped and cheaper than new ones. On the other hand, costs of heat, repairs and maintenance, especially when contracted out, can be double or triple those of new houses. In buying any home, your first consideration should be comfort: a solid house, concerned neighbors, and good community services. Hoped-for appreciation should always be secondary.

To get an idea of what you're getting into, talk with a lending institution in the area where you plan to live. Generally, the lender will limit the mortgage to fifteen years—about the actuarial life of a 65-year-old male.

You may be able to stretch the loan for a few more years, especially with a new house, but the key to the monthly cost will be the down payment. Typically, this will be a minimum of 20 percent.

Table 17–1 lists the costs per $1,000 loan when the interest rate is 16 percent and the term 15 years. Use this to:

1. Estimate monthly payments. With a $30,000 mortgage, you will pay $440.70 with a fifteen-year loan at 16 percent interest.

2. To calculate the loan you can afford with a specific monthly payment: $500 will support a fifteen-year mortgage of $34,036 at 16 percent; a twenty-year one of about $36,000.

Table 17–2 gives you a base for determining tax deductions for interest. In year 1, the write-off for that $30,000 mortgage is $4,761 a year; in year 3, it's down to $4,566; in year 10, to $3,090.

Keep in mind that these tables show costs with a conventional, flat payment mortgage and a fixed rate of interest with the institution assuming the risks of changes in the cost of money. But you may have to accept one of the new types of loans where the interest rate and/or monthly payment is flexible. With these, you assume the risks of money-cost changes. You may win if interest rates decline, but you will lose when they rise.

With all major financial commitments, such as a mortgage, look ahead and be certain that you will be able to meet the payments without stress. Do not let pride or status seeking lure you into buying a house you cannot afford.

Table 17-1.   Monthly Mortgage Payments   (per $1,000 Loan)

Mortgage Life	Percentages							
	14	14.50	15	15.50	16	16.50	17	17.50
10	$15.52	$15.83	$16.13	$16.44	$16.75	$17.06	$17.38	$17.70
15	13.32	13.65	13.99	14.34	14.69	15.04	15.39	15.74
20	12.44	12.80	13.17	13.54	13.91	14.29	14.67	15.05
25	12.04	12.42	12.81	13.20	13.59	13.98	14.38	14.77

NOTE: Use this table to estimate monthly cost of owning your house. The data include amortization. On a 10-year, $50,000 loan at 15%, check the first line to find the $16.13 base. Multiply by 50 to get a monthly payment of $806.50. This does not include such costs of insurance, real estate taxes, maintenance, etc.

SOURCE: David Thorndike, ed., *The Thorndike Encyclopedia of Banking and Financial Tables*, Warren, Gorham & Lamont, Boston, Mass., 1980.

Table 17–2.   Mortgage Amortization Schedule

(Monthly Payment for 15-year loan @ 16% per $100. Annual Constant: $16.14)

Year	Annual Interest	Annual Principal	Year-end Balance
1	$15.87	$ 1.75	$98.25
3	15.22	2.40	93.80
5	14.32	3.30	87.68
7	13.08	4.54	79.26
10	10.31	7.31	60.39
12	7.57	10.05	41.77
15	1.44	16.19	. . . . . .

SOURCE: David Thorndike, ed., *The Thorndike Encyclopedia of Banking and Financial Tables,* Warren, Gorham & Lamont, Boston, Mass., 1980.

18. Financing the Purchase
and Sale of a Home

Most older people are familiar with fixed interest, fixed payment mortgages, but increasingly, there are alternatives. A few of them benefit the
borrower, but most are designed to help the lender cope with the rapid
changes in the cost of money that have taken place in recent years and
appear likely to continue. One thing is sure: these new mortgages are
flexible.

Financing the Purchase

Here's a summary of the most popular innovations, but, chances are,
there will be further variations in the years ahead. More than ever
before, it is essential to get full information about the possible consequences. Some loans which appear attractive now can be onerous, if not
devastating, in the future. No one can predict how much money will
cost in the future. We hope that interest rates will decline, but there's
no guarantee that this will happen!

Always find out what you must pay ten or fifteen years from now.
If you are younger and still working, you should be able to adjust. But
if you're retired (or plan to retire soon) on a more or less fixed income,
you can have problems that may force you to lower your standard of
living.

Graduated Payment Mortgage (GPM)

With this, the payments for interest and amortization start low,
increase gradually for the next five or ten years and then level out on
terms of a standard mortgage.

What happens is that the modest down payment goes into an escrow
account where principal and interest are used to supplement the be-
low-normal payments for the first five years. By the time the "grace"
period is ended, the deposit will be nearly exhausted but the borrower,

presumably, will be making more money and able to afford the higher payments.

Over the full time-span of the mortgage, total payments will be about 10 percent greater than those of a conventional loan. Other variations call for escalating monthly payments and/or interest rates.

GPMs are not suitable for older people unless, through inheritance, a trust fund or redemption of assets, they can count on higher incomes five or ten years hence.

Variable Rate Mortgage (VRM)

With this, the interest rate moves with the cost of money as measured by an index outside the lender's control.

Generally, VRMs are offered at 0.25 percent below the institution's fixed mortgage rate and are guaranteed for the first year. Thereafter, the rate can be boosted every six months but no more than 0.25 percent at a time. There are no restrictions on the decrease if money costs decline. There's no penalty for prepayment and, if the house is resold, the lender can continue the loan at the then current interest rate.

VRMs are becoming increasingly popular with thrift institutions so will probably be the type of loan first suggested to you. A standard mortgage is still the best for those with more or less fixed incomes, but if you believe that interest rates will drop in the next few years, a VRM can assure substantial savings. Still, don't forget that when this happens, the returns on your short-term investments, such as Treasury bills and money market funds, will decline, too.

Renegotiable Rate Mortgage (RRM)

This is a variation of the VRM. In effect, the mortgage is a series of short-term (three- to five-year) renegotiable loans. The interest rate can be raised or lowered in line with the national mortgage rate index. The maximum annual shift is 0.5 percent with a limit of $\pm$ 5 percent over the life of the loan. When the cost of money declines, the rate *must* be lowered; when it rises, it *may* be increased.

Again, this is likely to be the format favored by the lender but a conventional mortgage, with its fixed terms, is better for older folks.

Shared Appreciation Mortgage

This is another gimmick designed to cope with inflation. It swaps a low interest rate for a share of future appreciation of the property. With

Advance Mortgage Corporation, here's how it works:

Tom R. buys an $80,000 house with $20,000 down and a $60,000 mortgage at an interest rate that is about one-third below the prevailing cost of money: say, 12 percent when loans carry 17 percent. Ten years hence, when Tom decides to move, he sells the home for $110,000, a gross profit of $30,000. Of this, Tom keeps two-thirds ($20,000) but must pay one-third ($10,000) to the financial firm.

This can be a good deal for families with modest income, but it may not be so favorable for those in a 50 percent tax bracket because:

1. The interest is deductible, so Uncle Sam pays half of this cost. The bigger the interest payments, the greater the tax benefits.

2. One-third of the appreciation may work out to be more than one-third of the lower interest paid.

3. If you use the ultimate proceeds to buy a new home, you may lose out on a tax-free rollover (when the new dwelling costs more than the old) and you may not have enough cash to make the down payment on the purchase.

Before signing for this type of loan, consult your tax adviser and have him project all costs and benefits at various levels of appreciation for the next ten years.

Mortgages-in-Law

These are a form of bank-financed construction loans adapted to new homes. They have been successful in several retirement communities.

Example: Bill C., newly retired, wants to buy a $70,000 home in Florida, but finds that Sam Meyerson, the potential buyer for his present $100,000 house cannot qualify at the then current 15 percent mortgage rate.

The builder gives Bill a ten-year mortgage at just under 16 percent for $60,000—the approximate amount of a conventional loan on the property. Bill makes this proposal to Sam: "Put up a $20,000 down payment, arrange for a $60,000 mortgage (for which you can qualify) and I'll take back a ten-year mortgage for the remaining $20,000 at a low 12 percent interest rate."

The deal is closed. Bill gets $80,000 cash. He uses $10,000 to buy the new home and invests the balance in shares of a money market fund, with a 12 percent yield. That gives him income of $10,400: $8,400 from the investment plus $2,000 a year interest on the second mortgage. If the rate of return falls, he will still have more than enough to pay off his own mortgage at maturity or arrange for a new loan.

Bill didn't get the highest return on his loan, but he buys the new home quickly, gets a relatively low rate of interest on the loan and beats inflation by repaying with ever worth-less dollars.

Reverse Mortgage

This is more or less an emergency source of money after retirement. It's expensive but it can provide income from an otherwise nonproductive asset. It's worthwhile for someone who wants to stay in his/her house for the next five to ten years, but it is seldom wise for those who hope to live in their homes indefinitely. As the name implies, it's a mortgage under which payments are made to the owner by the lending institution.

Here's a true case history that took place in 1979, when interest rates were "reasonable." Carol F., a 75-year-old widow was living on Social Security and income from dwindling savings. She enjoyed her home and community and did not want to move. From the local savings and loan association, she borrowed $64,000 (80 percent of the value of her home) for ten years at 10.5 percent interest. After deductions for interest, insurance, taxes, etc., she received a monthly check for $303.58— all she needed to live comfortably.

At the end of ten years, she would have to repay the $64,000, of which $27,750 would be interest. If the house continues to appreciate in value, she could roll over the mortgage and take out a new loan against the higher worth. If she dies before 1989, her executor would sell the house to satisfy the debt.

The danger, of course, is that she will live beyond age 85. At 10.5 percent interest, this reverse mortgage made sense but at 16 percent, it's probably a last resort. Still, when you are well in your 70s, money is not as important as peace of mind. Mrs. F. will be using her assets even though she will leave less to her children.

Sale/Leaseback

This is a form of reverse mortgage that can be a good deal for older people who are worried about living too long and for younger people able to afford a long-term investment. It was developed by The Fouratt Corporation in Carmel, California, a retirement haven.

The older couple sells their home at a discount from the present market value under a leaseback arrangement that permits them to remain in the house as long as either lives.

The buyer puts up 10 percent cash and agrees to pay all maintenance, property taxes and insurance plus a regular monthly check.

To assure full payment, the young buyer purchases an annuity for the old folks. In effect, this guarantees that the sellers can stay in the home even after equity payments are completed.

The buyer gets the eventual capital gain and deductions for the interest and, if IRS approves, for depreciation. This type of mortgage is expensive, but the retirees get income and a home for life.

Both of these types of reverse mortgages are useful with retirees whose children have investment funds. The loan protects their parent(s) and they receive a fair return. One of the recommendations of the White House Conference on Aging called for the development of some sort of insurance/guarantee program to make these mortgages more acceptable by enabling lending institutions to sell them off to provide funds for new loans.

Other Mortgages

There are other types of mortgages which, generally, are better for selling than buying. Two of the most widely used are:

Balloon Mortgage. This is a commercial type of mortgage that starts with a low monthly payment, usually figured on a twenty-five-year loan basis. Full payment is due in five or ten years.

For older borrowers, they are suitable only if you can count on extra funds by repayment time; *for older lenders,* they can be excellent investments when taken back at the sale of their home. They provide steady income and a big "bonus" when paid up.

Second Mortgage. Typically, this will yield 3 percent to 5 percent above current interest rates on home loans. It is most useful in selling your home because it can enable the buyer to qualify for a regular mortgage. These loans can also be rewarding investments.

Before you boast about the 20 percent-plus yields, do your homework. By definition, all second mortgages involve risks. Always double-check the financial resources of the borrower, review the contract with an attorney knowledgeable about real estate and protect your position by:

• Keeping the loan to a short period, not more than ten years.

• Setting penalties for late payments. If interest rates decline, the crafty borrower may delay payments so that you will have to foreclose. This can be expensive, time-consuming and worrisome.

- Recording the transaction in the county office with a notice of default. You will be informed if the buyer defaults on the first mortgage and be ready for probable foreclosure.
- Filing all receipts for payments to strengthen your case if a default ends in court.
- Including safety clauses for:

Acceleration. To give you the option, in the event of a resale, of continuing the second mortgage with the new buyer or demanding that the note be paid off in full before the property is sold.

Priority. To provide that there can be no increase in the first mortgage without your loan being paid off. Without such a provision, the borrower can refinance the first mortgage, get his down payment back, abandon the house and come out even . . . or better. You would have to assume the first mortgage or lose your entire investment.

Notification. That, in event of default on the first mortgage, you are willing to continue payments on it. In return, you must be notified in advance of the forthcoming foreclosure. If the borrower kept up his payments on the first mortgage and defaulted on the second, the property might be auctioned off and there might be nothing left for you.

Second mortgages may provide high returns but they can be dangerous, especially for retirees living in another area.

Zero Interest Mortgage (ZIM). This is another sales tool for new houses, but it can work out well for retirees who have ample cash. It requires about a 30 percent down payment, but there's no interest for five years. Since you won't own the property for sixty months, the closing costs are low.

Here's how ZIM compares with a conventional and FHA loan on a $60,000 home:

	ZIM	Conventional	FHA
Price of home	$60,000	$60,000	$60,000
Down payment	18,000	12,000	2,500
Closing costs	200	1,800	3,000
Total cash outlay	18,200	13,800	5,500
Amount financed	42,000	48,000	57,500
Interest rate	0	17.5%	16.5%
Monthly payments	700	704	797
Interest after 5 years	0	41,856	47,303
Equity after 5 years	42,000	384	517
Plus down payment	60,000	12,384	3,017

This is a good example of how expensive mortgages can be. With a 16.5 percent interest rate, you "repay" the loan every 4⅓ years; at 12 percent, every six years. To make your own calculations, use the rule of 72: divide 72 by the interest rate.

But the net cost can be less depending on your tax bracket because that interest is tax deductible.

Repaying/Refinancing Your Own Mortgage

When you have an old, low-interest mortgage, repayment/refinancing usually makes sense, in dollars, only under two conditions: when (1) you need money (see chap. 11) or; (2) you are nearing retirement and expect to be in such a low tax bracket that the deductions for interest will not be meaningful (by this time, the write-offs will probably be small anyway).

But if you will sleep better when you are debt free, take advantage of any money-savings opportunities. Always do your homework first. The lending institution will make an offer only when it is to its own benefit!

Example: Dan S. has an 8 percent mortgage with a balance of $19,146.63. His friendly savings and loan makes this pitch: "With your current monthly payments of $171.35, it will take 206 more payments to repay the loan. You will pay $16,151.47 in interest.

"If you agree to double your payments to $342.70, we will reduce your interest rate to 7 percent and the loan can be paid off in 71 months. The interest payments will be reduced by $5,185.07."

O.K., but now get out your calculator. If you took the extra $171.35 a month and invested it at 12 percent, after 71 months, you could pay off the mortgage and pocket $1,200. At this point, there would be no more deductions for the interest.

But if you continue to work for 206 months (17 years), you would be better off to keep the old loan and take the tax deductions.

Financing the Sale

When you sell your house, you may have to utilize what is known as "creative financing." In most cases, this will be needed when the prospective buyer is unable to come up with the necessary cash down payment or to qualify for loans from institutional lenders. It may take a little work but there are almost always ways to finance a sale.

FHA or VA Mortgage

If you have one of these mortgages, you're in luck because: (1) all of these loans are assumable by a new buyer; (2) a qualified buyer is eligible for financing of up to 95 percent of the value of the house to a maximum of $98,500; (3) a qualified seller can trade in his present loan for a new one up to 90 percent of current value to the same maximum.

All arrangements can be made through a local thrift institution which will also handle the bookwork for 1 percent of the mortgage balance in the first year and 0.5 percent annually thereafter. And, most important, if you continue to hold the mortgage, you can sell it to the bank at some future date.

The amount and interest rate of these new loans are almost always below prevailing rates. They will be based on the unpaid balance, the old interest rate and the number of years remaining on the loan, plus the amount and term of the new mortgage.

Two examples: Dan M. has a 9.5 percent mortgage which was sold by the original lender to the Federal National Mortgage Association (FNMA). The house is worth $85,000; the unpaid balance of the loan is $50,208.

You offer to defray part of the buyer's mortgage payments when he makes an escrow deposit. Rather than drop the price of your house by $4,800, you agree to pay the buyer $200 per month for two years (so he gets his money back). You make money by investing the cash; at 12 percent, compounded daily, you'll earn over $1,300.

Or you rent your house with an option to buy. Typically, this involves a $2,000 "commitment fee" which you keep if the option is not exercised. Again, you get that all-important interest.

Wraparound Mortgage

This is a fancy second mortgage which "wraps around" the old mortgage with a new loan. It's a good way to sell your house and receive a steady income. But it does require some bookkeeping.

Example (based on an actual case history when interest rates were lower): Charlie B. was ready to retire and move out of state. His home was worth $100,000; the mortgage, a 9 percent VA loan, was paid down to $40,000. Charlie sold for $15,000 cash, plus a $85,000 wraparound mortgage at 12 percent.

The buyer agreed to make the monthly payments to Charlie who continued to pay off the original loan. He received $10,200 a year. From this, he paid $3,600 on the old loan, netting $6,600, a 14.67 percent return on the $45,000 investment at risk. Dan can refinance his mortgage with a new loan of $70,000 at 10.875 percent. Now, the monthly payment will be upped from $379 to $660, but Dan can invest $25,000 to earn $3,000 every year to almost bridge the gap.

Jonas B. wants to sell his house which has a 7.5 percent mortgage, also owned by FNMA. It is paid down to $22,285. He receives $2,650 cash from the buyer, who takes out a $50,000 mortgage at 12.6 percent. The buyer's monthly payment will be $538—$95 less than that of a new 15 percent conventional loan.

Taking Back a Mortgage

This can be done either with the assumption of the original mortgage or through a new loan plus a second mortgage held by the seller. To be on the safe side, this should require a substantial down payment, and on the second loan fast repayment (five to ten years) and a competitive, or higher, rate of interest.

You do sell the house but you also have to assume the risks of a secondary position. This can provide steady income during retirement but, in most cases, it's a frozen asset. If you need money in a hurry, you will have to sell the second mortgage at a substantial discount. This is calculated by taking the desired yield, say 20 percent, and dividing the sum of the yield and the fraction of one over the term of the mortgage.

Example: Charlie C. takes back a $10,000 second mortgage, due in five years, at 17 percent. Soon after, he needs money. A lender might offer about $8,400, a return of 20 percent on the $8,400 investment.

These examples point out that the homeowner has a number of options in financing a purchase or sale of his home. For older people, the best mortgage is the standard loan with fixed terms, but if this is not available, select the new type that best fits your resources, income and mental attitude. With the right kind of house in a good location, you can count on appreciation so that, if you do run into trouble, you can refinance at a tax-free profit.

As you near or pass retirement age, you will realize that there may be good and bad times to buy a *house* but not a *home.* If you like the place and can afford to keep it, do not hesitate to buy. Maybe you can get a lower price or better terms, but the few dollars saved won't offset the lost pleasure of ownership.

And the older you get, the more cautious you should become. A mortgage is a fixed expense that must be paid every month. With limited income and inflated costs, this outlay can become burdensome and cramp your lifestyle. Do not become house poor.

Moving is difficult at any age, but, financially, for most retirees, it will probably be the most rewarding decision. You can cash in on the high sale price, pay little or no taxes and put more of your assets to work to provide income to do all those things you have dreamed of for so many years.

Home Improvements Before Selling

With a major asset such as your home, the judicious expenditure of a few dollars for cleaning, painting and modernizing can boost the sale price substantially. But be cautious about major expenditures. In most cases, such changes will reflect your own (and spouse's) ideas and may not appeal to buyers who have trouble enough coming up with the necessary money and tend to shy away from costly "improvements" they do not control.

A good way to check the value of costly improvements is to get a written statement from a knowledgeable real estate agent. Such action won't guarantee a higher price, but it will stimulate greater sales efforts.

As a rule of thumb, every $1,000 expenditure should increase the house value by 2.12 percent. That is, if you spend $2,000 on a separate family room, you should get at least $4,240 more on the sale.

The benefits of improvements depend on the type and condition of your house. If the exterior is flaking and weather blotched, a coat of paint is important. But unless the interior walls and molding are scuffed and faded, it will not be worthwhile to repaint inside. The new owners will have their own ideas of color combinations that best suit their furniture.

It's wise to present an attractive package but do not make everything so spic and span that the house looks as if it has never been lived in. Cut the lawn close to make weeds and crabgrass less apparent; add inexpensive shrubs and colorful flowers to sparkle the landscaping; clean the basement; and straighten out the attic.

To create the feeling that you have cared for the home, replace all outdated electrical switches and outlets; add a fire/smoke detector; install a garbage disposal unit and, if you live in a wintry area, consider double glass windows. None of these are expensive (if you can do the work yourself) when compared to the extra $500 you may get. Besides, they will make your own living more comfortable.

Other major improvements—swimming pool, screened porch, etc. —seldom pay off. They represent what you wish you had done, not what the buyer may want. Use that added-on formula and do not spend money without encouragement from your agent. You want to end up with more, not less, money.

Finally, keep in mind that no matter how lovely and attractive you may feel the house is, the ultimate price will reflect the neighborhood. When most homes sell for less than $100,000, you will have a tough time getting much more regardless of how many improvements you make.

Epilogue:
Relax, Be Useful and Happy

In the final analysis, all the financial planning will make for security but not happiness. Money takes the pressures off, but with unfilled days and no focus, life will be dreary and dull—even in the sparkling southern sun.

In other words, more than *financial* planning and financial security is needed for retirement. Retire *to* something, not just from a job. Think of retirement as the ultimate promotion, the start of a new, exciting, rewarding experience, where there can be freedom of thought and action that previously was impossible.

Herewith, then, is a summary of some dos and don'ts and a good checklist of all we've been talking about in this book.

Well Before Retirement

Do get an early start on financial planning. Money will always be a necessity, but it's the sugar that sweetens life and makes possible the little treats we all dream of and need: travel, dinners out, gifts to someone special or tickets to a show.

Start your pension plan(s) as soon as you can with as much as you can. If you are able to contribute only $10 a week in the early years, do it. After college bills are paid, you will be able to boost those savings. In just ten years, that $2,000 a year will compound to enough to assure extra, annual lifetime income of $5,000—more if you invade capital.

Don't delay joining or setting up a pension plan. To build a $100,000 nest egg for retirement at age 65, with a 12 percent annual rate of return, in a tax-advantaged retirement fund requires a yearly contribution of $5,089 for ten years; $1,239 for twenty years.

Do write the first check, every month, to yourself: for your retirement plan. After the agony of the first few months, you'll adjust and never (well, almost never) miss it.

With consistent savings and prompt reinvestment of all income, a

$2,000 per year investment (available for everyone with the new Individual Retirement Account), earning 12 percent with compounding, will grow to $39,930 in ten years; to $161,400 in twenty years. These savings can provide lifetime income of $4,800 to over $20,000, respectively, a year. Even with inflation, these sums will be meaningful.

With wise investing, you can always stay ahead of inflation. The soaring inflation of the past few years is temporary. In this century, inflation has averaged under 3 percent a year; since 1950, that average rose to over 4 percent despite the pressures, of the oil crisis and high interest rates. Now it is declining and over the long-term of pension building and spending can be expected to average well under 5 percent a year. Profitable investments will provide higher rates of return and with few or no taxes, most retirees will do O.K.

Nearing Retirement

Do set up a timetable. In your 50s, get your finances in shape; start discussions on retirement with your spouse, your family and your friends who are no longer working.

In your 60s, clean up long-term debts, arrange for a smooth transition by replacing old appliances, buying a new car and selling or giving away unneeded possessions. Consider whether you want to stay in your home or move and, if so, where.

Do start shifting your lifestyle gradually: developing new sources of income; taking lessons if you plan to paint or make ceramics; establishing outside interests with which you can enjoyably occupy your time in future years; limiting social and volunteer commitments.

Do establish individual credit for both husband and wife: with retail stores, credit card companies and banks while you are working and can count on references. If you plan to move, set up accounts at banks and stores in the new area when you make your first deposit on your new home.

Do test out the new living area: visit in both winter and summer or rent for several months. Subscribe to a local newspaper and make it a point to talk with neighbors and friends.

Do have something to look forward to: new places to visit; new hobbies to try; new books to read; new recipes to test. When you stop being active and start feeling sorry for yourself, you're in trouble.

Do agree on early retirement. If one spouse is not 100 percent in favor of it, forget it. After work, you will be enjoying(?) home/life together.

After Retirement

Do retire into something. It may take some hard thinking and self-discipline at first, but now is the time to pursue those projects you never had time for.

Don't change your way of life without due consideration. If you sell the old homestead and run off to Florida, six months later, you both may wish you had the old place back.

Do go slow on buying a business or franchise. This can take a good chunk of your savings and the mortality rate for such enterprises is incredibly high.

Do remember you are growing older. Most people over 65 start to slow down physically and, to some degree, in lifestyle. They eat less, drive less and play less.

At 70, few men and women can play golf more than twice a week and fewer are willing to endure the rigors of long trips. At 75, most folks will be lucky to be able to play golf more than once a week and to enjoy one major annual "vacation."

Don't plan on long trips after five to eight years of retirement. One, or both, of you will become itchy after being away a month (or less). One spouse will want to get back to the weekly golf game, the other will worry about the roof leaking or the air conditioner going on the blink.

Don't place safety of your investments above all else. The safest investments are obligations of the U.S. Government but savings and retirement bonds pay minimum interest and are worth less every year because of inflation. A-rated corporate bonds pay well, and you'll always get your money back at maturity. Common stocks of quality corporations and well-located real estate will grow in income and value.

Don't get locked in with your investments. In 1978, the highest yields from a thrift account was 8 percent with an eight-year certificate of deposit. In 1979, the rate of return for a six-month CD was over 15 percent.

Furthermore, the purchasing power of fixed income holdings, such as bonds and mortgages, is eroded by inflation. After ten years, with 5 percent inflation, every $1,000 will buy only $784 of the same goods and services.

Do stay flexible with your savings: an emergency cache in a low-yielding NOW or savings account; a modest amount in high yielding money market funds or CDs; and the balance in a mix of bonds bought at a discount and actively traded, quality stocks or shares of mutual funds.

Don't hoard your capital with the idea that you will beat the averages of your life span projections: for a 65-year-old male, 14 years (to age 79); for a female, 18 years (to age 83); for a 72-year-old male, 10.1 years (82); female, 13.4 years (85). These averages reflect actuarial experience so half will die earlier and half will live longer. If your female ancestors were long-lived, add 5 years.

Do take advantage of the benefits of retirement: discounts for transportation, drugs, entertainment, car rentals, hotels/motels, vacation attractions, and educational opportunities.

Do get out of step with the working world: go shopping between 10 A.M. and 3 P.M.; travel Monday through Thursday; vacation off season.

Do become a good shopper: watch for special sales; use coupons for items you NEED; stock up several months when standard foods are advertised at seasonally low prices.

Don't shelter your wife from financial facts. In most cases, the woman will outlive the man. If she does not know, and understand, family finances, there can be severe problems.

Do decide who is to handle the money and make sure that each partner knows and respects this responsibility.

Don't retain too much life insurance. After age 65, keep only enough to meet final death expenses. Be wary of trusts as, in most cases, they are no longer needed to save taxes . . . unless you are wealthy.

Don't be gypped by get-rich-quick schemes, prize contests that require you to put up money, sympathy sales such as "I'm working my way through college," quack cures for arthritis, etc., and "easy" ways to earn money at home: raising mushrooms, typing manuscripts, addressing envelopes, and so forth.

Don't worry unduly about costs of catastrophic illness. Eighty-nine percent of all people over age 65 escape such problems. The remaining 11 percent include all those who were already in nursing homes or institutions. And, chances are, Congress will enact some form of catastrophic medical/health insurance.

Do be willing to spend part of your capital after a few years of retirement. You can stop at any time and revert to your former spending habits.

Do remember that you are retired so there's no need to rush or to finish each task the day you started it.

Do paste this at the top of your mirror and read it every morning:
TODAY IS THE FIRST DAY OF THE REST OF MY LIFE

Financial Checklist

IF YOU RETIRE IN 1982:

	Husband	Wife	Total
	Monthly		Annual
Social Security	$604	$302	$10,872
Employer pension			2,800
Savings/investments			3,500
Investment of portion of proceeds of sale of home			2,400
Total retirement income			$19,572

IF YOU RETIRE IN 10 YEARS:

Present: both age 55

	Husband	Wife	Total
Salary/wages	$25,000	$10,000	$35,000
Investments			3,500
Total income			$38,500

With retirement at age 65, 10 years to go for:

	Husband	Wife	Total
Last working year's income	$35,000	$15,000	$50,000
Retirement income goal:	@ 60%	@ 75%	
	$30,000	$37,500	

Retirement income:	Husband	Wife	
Social Security @ 5% annual increase	$966	$483	$17,388
Employer pension			4,200
Personal pension (IRA)			4,800
Investments			4,000
Investments from sale of home			3,600
Total			$33,988

Major Expenses in Last 5 Years of Work

Item	Estimated Cost	Your Cost
Automobile (with trade-in)	$ 5,000	_____
Appliances:		
Refrigerator	1,200	_____
Washer	500	_____
Dryer	500	_____
Air conditioning	500	_____
Television	400	_____
Stereo	1,000	_____
Furniture	3,000	_____
Miscellaneous	900	_____
Total	$13,000	
Purchase Schedule:		
Year 5	$ 4,000	
Year 4	3,000	
Year 3	2,500	
Year 2	2,000	
Year 1	1,500	
	$13,000	

Index

About the Author

C. Colburn Hardy writes with firsthand knowledge of retirement and its financing before and after work.

Retirement: He has been retired from formal work for eleven years and started a second career as a writer, has lived in an adult community, served as chairman of the Palm Beach County delegation to the White House Conference on Aging, and, recently, was named by Governor Bob Graham to the Florida Council on Aging and Adult Services.

Pension Plans: As financial editor of Physician's Management, he has written scores of articles on retirement plans.

Money Management: He has been editor of the annual *Dun & Bradstreet's Guide to Your Investments* since 1974 and author of three books on investments and personal money management.

Mr. Hardy is a 1931 Phi Beta Kappa graduate of Yale, and has been a newspaper publisher, two-term member of the New Jersey Legislature, a Naval Air Combat Intelligence Officer during World War II, and a public relations executive with nationally known agencies and corporations.

He has written over 1,400 articles, taught at colleges, lectured at seminars, and appeared on national and local radio and TV programs. As described by one reviewer, "Colburn Hardy does his homework and presents information in terms that readers can understand and use."